CLINICAL SKILLS
for
MEDICAL STUDENTS:
A HANDS-ON GUIDE

PASTEST
Dedicated to your success

CLINICAL SKILLS for MEDICAL STUDENTS: A HANDS-ON GUIDE

Ian Bickle
Queen's University Belfast

Paul Hamilton BSc
Queen's University Belfast

David McCluskey MD, FRCP, FRCPI
Head of Department of Medicine,
Queen's University Belfast

Barry Kelly MD, FRCS, FRCR, FFRRCSI
Consultant Radiologist,
Royal Victoria Hospital, Belfast

PASTEST
Dedicated to your success

© 2001 PasTest Ltd

Egerton Court
Parkgate Estate
Knutsford
Cheshire, WA16 8OX

Telephone: 01565 752000

First edition 2001

ISBN: 1 901198 86 3

A catalogue record for this book is available from the British Library.

The information contained within this book was obtained by the authors from reliable sources. However, while every effort has been made to ensure its accuracy, no responsibility for loss, damage or injury occasioned to any person acting or refraining from action as a result of information contained herein can be accepted by the publisher or the authors.

PasTest Revision Books and Intensive Courses
PasTest has been established in the field of postgraduate medical education since 1972, providing revision books and intensive study courses for doctors preparing for their professional examinations. Books and courses are available for the following specialties:
Undergraduate exams, MRCP Part 1 and Part 2, MRCPCH Part 1 and Part 2, MRCOG, DRCOG, MRCGP, MRCPsych, DCH, FRCA, MRCS and PLAB.

For further details contact:

PasTest Ltd, Freepost, Knutsford, Cheshire, WA16 7BR
Tel: 01565 752000   Fax: 01565 650264
Email: enquiries@pastest.co.uk   **Web site: www. pastest.co.uk**

Typeset by Saxon Graphics Ltd, Derby
Printed by Bell and Bain Ltd, Glasgow

Contents

Acknowledgements

This book on practical clinical skills has been carefully produced with the medical student in mind. It is for this reason that we hope you find it applicable and focused to your needs. Our intentions were to produce something that students would turn to on a regular basis because it is easy to follow, concise and useful to everyday practice.

It is doubtful that anyone could develop their own clinical skills without the instruction and demonstration by more experienced colleagues. This is why we would encourage you to ask someone if you don't understand a particular test or aspect of an examination. We have sought, and will continue to seek, the advice and skills of more senior medics. For this reason it is only proper that we acknowledge all those who have instructed and taught us across Northern Ireland's hospitals. A special thanks goes to all the staff at the Clinical Skills Centre at Belfast City Hospital, a comforting and ideal learning environment from the earliest days of our medical education.

The clarity and readability of this text owes much to Mary McCaffery and Glen Clarke, who constructively criticised all aspects. Their attention to clinical detail and examination layout is greatly appreciated.

The most important thank you goes to many people who may never know of our gratitude. A group of people, whom during times of trouble in unfamiliar environments, spare their time, patience and good nature – **the patients**.

Introduction

"To study the phenomena of disease without books is to sail an uncharted sea. Whilst to study books without patients is not to go to sea at all."

Sir William Osler (1840–1919)

Clinical skills are the basis on which medical practice operates, and, despite technological advancements, are still the foundation of patient-based medicine. This book details the key examinations especially relevant to the medical student. All chapters refer to examination of the adult patient. Techniques are explained in an easy to follow format, which, while being ideal for the newcomer to clinical examination, will also serve as a ready reference and revision guide for more advanced students. The book does not aim to be extensive in covering all clinical examinations; nor does it detail every possible aspect of each specific examination – it is a practical guide to **essential** clinical skills.

The format is designed to be accessible to all students and combines practicality with foundation knowledge in examining body systems. Major system examinations such as cardiovascular and respiratory are included, along with other frequently examined regions such as the breast and thyroid gland.

> ***You will also note the use of the boxes that emphasize essential parts of the examination which in some cases can be easily missed – not least with the nerves of an assessment situation.***

You should think about any clinical examination you carry out in the context of what we call the 'GOLDEN TRIANGLE':

1. Why the procedure is being carried out
2. How to do the procedure
3. Applying anatomical knowledge

This triangle permits the application of knowledge and common sense in carrying out a useful rather than idealistic but impractical examination.

A difficulty for most students, particularly in the early days of patient contact, is approaching patients with the confidence to carry out an examination. Although examining real patients with real pathology is the most fruitful experience, it is often valuable to practise certain routines on a willing friend or family member, until they become second nature.

Golden Triangle

You will notice that experienced clinicians can tailor a particular examination to the requirements of the patient. You should therefore use this book to provide you with a framework which can be fallen back on. A methodical approach is needed that is flexible enough to undertake specific components as assessment or hospital circumstances dictate.

Don't rely on examinations on their own! It is important to remember that the clinical examination is no substitute for a quality history which can provide over 70% of all information on which the diagnosis is based. For this purpose, a chapter is included detailing how to document a medical case, including the core questions for each system. You should carry out all examinations with the history you have elicited in mind – this will confirm or clarify your suspicions and detect additional or incidental findings. The history should be taken first where possible.

We hope that you will find this book both useful and enjoyable.

Ian Bickle, Paul Hamilton,   **Queen's University Belfast.**

Knowledge acquired through reading is essential in medicine but inevitably some of what is read is eventually forgotten and often has to be relearned. Knowledge acquired through direct patient contact, reinforced with textbook reading, is often retained for life and serves as an invaluable learning experience for clinicians. For this reason, clinical case history recording is frequently used in general medicine, surgery and the specialties as an educational experience for students.

Chapter 8, Medical Records and Case Documentation, outlines the methods for the obtaining a structured clinical history, and describes a scheme for the documentation of clinical case histories and physical findings.

A good case history is one that combines accuracy and attention to detail, with clarity and conciseness.

With time and experience you can become more selective about which details of history and physical examination need to be recorded. Initially, however, it is a sound educational experience to go through a systematic approach to history and examination until a sufficient level of clinical knowledge has been attained.

A case history is documented as an example of the layout and standard attainable by medical students in the clinical years.

Medical records used in the ward units are hand written and students need to practise the standard scheme for recording such notes.

Dr D R McCluskey MD, FRCP, FRCPI
Head of Department
Department of Medicine
Institute of Clinical Science
Queen's University Belfast

General Approach to the Patient

There are a number of simple, yet fundamental, points that need to be borne in mind when formally examining a patient.

- In examination circumstances, always conform to a professional appearance e.g. with regard to style of hair and clothing.
- Male students should be accompanied by a female chaperone when examining female patients (especially breast and pelvic examinations).
- Always introduce yourself to every patient stating your name and status. Shaking a patient's hand helps to build up a rapport.
- Before examining a patient, explain what will be involved in the examination, and ask for consent.
- Ensure that the patient is as comfortable as possible, in what may be an unfamiliar or daunting environment.
- Always pay attention to hygiene e.g. washing hands before and after examining a patient, and wearing gloves when necessary.
- Have short fingernails – long nails make percussion and palpation harder for you, and unpleasant for the patient.
- Examine from the right side of the patient except when this is not feasible.
- Ask if the body part to be examined is painful.
- If you are aware that a test is uncomfortable, or if you need the patient to be relaxed, employ distraction tactics, e.g. chat to the patient about something pleasant.
- Adequate exposure is essential, as is the patient's dignity. Therefore, provide something (e.g. blanket or gown) to temporarily cover the patient.
- Always examine and compare similar structures on both sides of the body, even if you know only one side is abnormal.
- Warm your hands or any object (e.g. stethoscope, tuning fork, speculum) that you are about to place on the patient's skin.
- When using a stethoscope, tap on the diaphragm to check it is not switched to the bell.
- When measuring, ensure that the measurement is accurately reproducible by recording distance from a fixed bony landmark.
- Listen to what the patient says, and respect their opinions at all times, they are often right.
- Thank the patient at the end of an examination.

General Inspection of the Patient

When a patient presents to a doctor, it is not always clear which system is responsible for the symptoms they complain of. In this regard, general inspection may guide you in your history and further examination. Although each examination begins with inspection of elements specific to that particular system or region, a prudent examiner should be aware of all aspects of a patient's demeanour. This chapter outlines some of the basic observations that you may wish to consider when engaging in any patient consultation. The level of detail that you go into will depend on the nature and location of the examination (hospital inpatient, outpatient or in General Practice). Often, many of these features will be noted subconsciously when dealing with a patient.

This part of the examination begins as soon as you meet the patient and is largely done through observation whilst taking the history.

State of illness

- Where does the patient fit on the spectrum from well to pre-morbid?

Colour

- Anaemic (pale)
- Cyanotic (blue lips of central cyanosis) and/or extremities (peripheral cyanosis)
- Jaundiced (yellow)
- Uraemic (grey)
- Flushed (pink)
- Polycythaemic (ruddy)
- Drug induced pigmentation (e.g. purple following chlorpromazine therapy)

Odour

Does an apparent smell greet you as you speak to the patient?
- Recreational activities: alcohol, tobacco, marijuana
- Hepatic foetor (stale urine/ammonia)
- Uraemic foetor (mice)
- Diabetic ketoacidosis (sweet/acetone)
- Otherwise malodorous (excess sweating, poor hygiene)

Hydration and nutrition

- Skin turgor, muscle bulk, oedema, moistness of mucous membranes
- Cachexic, anorexic, normal weight, overweight, obese

Attire

- Well groomed or unkempt
- Appropriateness of dress for the time, place and environment
- Spectacles/contact lenses/intraocular lenses
- Hearing aid/cochlear implant
- Laryngeal voice box
- Walking aids: walking stick, delta-rolator, Zimmer frame, white stick (if blind)

Facial appearance

There are many specific facial signs; several of which are indicative of a particular disease process, for example:

- Malar flush (mitral stenosis)
- Butterfly rash (SLE)
- Temporalis wasting (myotonic dystrophy)
- Lack of facial expression (Parkinson's disease)
- Moon face (Cushing's syndrome)
- Coarse features with a large mandible (acromegaly)
- Tight skin, pinched nose, small mouth (scleroderma)

Speech

Is there anything unusual about how the patient talks, for example:

- Hoarseness (e.g. in laryngitis)
- 'Donald duck' speech (in pseudobulbar palsy)
- Dysarthria, dysphasia, dysphonia
- Are they educationally limited?

Position and posture

- Do they need to sit up or lie down?
- Are they in pain?
- Are there any involuntary or abnormal movements (tremor, tics, fasciculation, writhing)?
- Do they limp on entering the room?
- Is there abnormal kyphosis/lordosis/scoliosis?

Body structure

Are any of the following apparent from external appearance:

- Mastectomy
- Amputation +/- prostheses
- False eye
- Toupee
- Tracheostomy
- Prominent dermatological conditions e.g. port wine stain

Objects and belongings

- 'Medic-Alert' bracelet
- Tobacco products
- Catheter bag on edge of bed
- Diabetic insulin pens, GTN spray, inhalers by bedside
- Sputum container. Note the colour of any sputum: white frothy (pulmonary oedema); green/yellow (infection); blood (haemoptysis)
- Nebuliser, oxygen mask/intranasal prongs, sputum cup(s), nutrient drinks
- Sleeping arrangements: 'ripple' bed, number of pillows; are they in an isolated room
- Evidence of hospital treatment, e.g. IV line in situ, chest drain, central venous line

Hospital records

- Temperature, respiratory rate, pulse, blood pressure, fluid input/output charts
- Capillary refill time, weight, Body Mass Index (BMI).

✓ *These may be provided by nursing staff or by examiners in an assessment scenario. ASK FOR THEM.*

There are potentially many more features that you may notice on passively or actively observing a patient during a medical consultation – this list is far from complete. Findings picked up in this way may help explain a good deal of the patient's symptomatology.

INSPECTION

- Inspect from the end of the bed
- Look for: malar flush, xanthelasma and corneal arcus
- Note the breathing pattern (*as in Respiratory System examination*), and look for obvious anaemia, cyanosis or jaundice.

Hands

- Look for: finger clubbing, signs of anaemia, peripheral cyanosis, evidence of smoking, tendon xanthomata. Stigmata of infective endocarditis (splinter haemorrhages, Osler's nodes, Janeway lesions, petechiae).

Three cardiac causes of finger clubbing

- Cyanotic heart disease
- Infective endocarditis
- Atrial myxoma

Examine the radial pulse

- When feeling for a pulse, it is often helpful to use two fingers. The distal finger (i.e. the one furthest away from the heart) can be pressed slightly harder, thus 'amplifying' the pulse transmitted to the other finger.

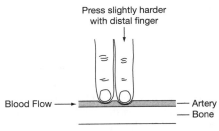

Technique for assessing a pulse

There are several features of a pulse which are important to note.

Important features of a pulse

- Rate (beats per minute)
- Rhythm (regular, regularly irregular, irregularly irregular)
- Character (e.g. normal, collapsing)
- Volume (normal, high, low)
- Vessel wall characteristics (normal, thickened)
- Symmetry (symmetrical, asymmetrical)

- Compare the pulse on both sides and note symmetry
- Feel the pulse on one side. Keep your hands in the same position, and elevate the patient's arm above their head. Abnormal pulsation may be felt with a 'water hammer' or 'collapsing' pulse – a characteristic of aortic regurgitation.

Measure blood pressure

- The patient should be as relaxed as possible, and should have been resting for some time before the measurement. Blood pressure is usually measured seated.
- Choose a suitably sized cuff, and wrap it securely around the patient's arm. Palpate the brachial artery in the antebrachial fossa, and adjust the cuff position so that it is in the correct position. (There is usually a mark on the cuff which should be lined up with the brachial artery).

> ✓ *The sphygmomanometer should be placed at the level of the heart.*

- Close the valve on the sphygmomanometer
- Palpate the pulse in the radial artery, and inflate the cuff to about 30 mmHg above the level at which the pulse disappears.
- Auscultate over the brachial artery with the stethoscope diaphragm
- Partly open the valve, so that the cuff pressure falls at a rate of about 2 mmHg per second

- Note the pressure at which you begin to hear rhythmical noises. These noises are Korotkoff sounds, and the pressure noted represents systolic blood pressure.
- Note the pressure at which the sounds disappear. This represents diastolic blood pressure. If the sounds do not disappear, the pressure at which they become muffled should be noted. The measurement should be repeated at least once, to improve accuracy.
- Compare the pressure with the patient sitting and after two minutes of standing. A systolic change of more than 20 mmHg between positions is indicative of postural hypotension.

Measure jugular venous pressure (JVP)

> ✓ *Adjust the bed so that the patient is lying at 45° to the horizontal.*

- Ask the patient to look over their left shoulder
- Ensure the area over the internal jugular vein is well illuminated (use a lamp)
- Look carefully for any pulsations
- Verify that pulsations are not arterial (by checking for the JVP features listed in the box below)
- The level of the JVP should be noted as in the diagram, by measuring the vertical height between the Angle of Louis and the top of the venous column (normal < 3 cm).
- Check for hepatojugular reflux: while closely watching the patient's neck, gradually apply firm pressure on the abdomen, and hold for 4–5 seconds. A rise in the position of pulsation is indicative of a positive reflux. Ask the patient if there is any pain or tenderness before doing this, and tell the patient to breathe normally during the test.

Features of a JVP

- Pulsations cannot be palpated
- Can be easily occluded
- Fills from above
- Has at least 2 positive wave-forms
- Varies with respiration, posture and hepatojugular reflux

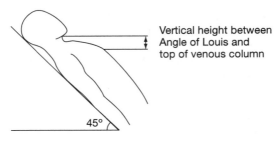

Vertical height between
Angle of Louis and
top of venous column

45°

Noting the level of the JVP

PRAECORDIUM (CHEST)

Inspect

- Look for any scars which might indicate previous cardiac surgery. These include: median sternotomy scars (coronary artery bypass or valve surgery), and lateral thoracotomy (mitral valve surgery in older patients).
- Look for any abnormal pulsation.

Palpate

- Apex beat (the most lateral and inferior position in which the heart can be palpated). Note the position of the apex beat in anatomical terms e.g. 5th intercostal space (ICS), mid-clavicular line.
- Heaves (forceful ventricular contractions)
- Thrills (palpable murmurs)

Hand positions for palpating heaves and thrills are shown in the diagram opposite.

Reasons for an impalpable apex beat on the left side

- Obesity
- Extreme muscle bulk
- Lung hyperinflation
- Dextrocardia
- Poor technique

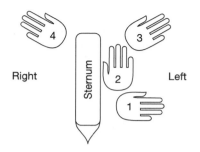

Hand positions for palpating heaves and thrills. Numbers indicate the order in which the positions may be used

Auscultation of the heart

✓ *Always palpate the carotid pulse when auscultating.*

- With the patient lying normally on the bed, auscultate in the mitral valve area with the stethoscope bell, as shown in the diagram. Roll the patient onto their left side. Relocate the apex beat, and auscultate the apex beat and axilla with the bell of the stethoscope. Listen specifically for the murmur of mitral stenosis.

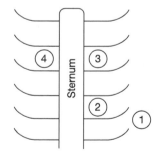

1: Mitral area   – Apex Beat
2: Tricuspid area   – Left 4th ICS
3: Pulmonary area – Left 2nd ICS
4: Aortic area   – Right 2nd ICS

Main areas for auscultation with diaphragm of stethoscope

- Roll the patient onto their back again. Auscultate the four valve areas with the stethoscope diaphragm.
- Ask the patient to lean forward off the bed, to exhale and hold their breath. Quickly auscultate over the tricuspid and aortic areas (for right-sided murmurs). Listen specifically for the murmur of aortic regurgitation.

- During auscultation, listen for normal heart sounds, extra heart sounds (3rd, 4th, clicks and prosthetic noises) and any other abnormalities. Distinguish systolic from diastolic abnormalities by noting the relationship of the abnormality with the pulse. If the abnormality occurs when you feel a pulse, it is a systolic problem. If it occurs when there is no pulse, it is a diastolic problem.
- Listen over the lung bases for inspiratory crepitations, which might be present in heart failure.
- Auscultate the carotid arteries for bruits with the diaphragm. Ensure the patient holds their breath first.
- You may also wish to auscultate over the abdominal aorta and renal arteries for bruits (*see Alimentary System Examination page 20*).

Assess the peripheral pulses

- Palpate the brachial (in the **antecubital fossa**), femoral (in the **groin**), popliteal (in the **popliteal fossa**), posterior tibial (posterior to the **medial malleolus at the ankle)** and dorsalis pedis **(on the top of the foot in line with the second toe)** pulses.
- Palpate the radial and femoral pulses, at the same time. A significant delay between the two is called radio-femoral delay, and is indicative of coarctation of the aorta.

Test for pitting oedema

- Press on the anterior aspect of the ankle for up to one minute. Release your finger, and inspect for 'pitting.' This may be present in right-sided heart failure.

Palpation of the liver may also reveal features such as enlargement in right heart failure, or pulsation in tricuspid regurgitation (*see Alimentary System Examination page 16*).

GENERAL EXAMINATION

> ✓ *Inspect from the end of the bed with the patient positioned at 45°, with the chest exposed.*

- Look for:
  signs of respiratory distress (e.g. use of accessory muscles)
  chest/abdominal movements during respiration
  obvious anaemia
  cyanosis
  iatrogenic Cushing's syndrome
  inspect the pattern of breathing and look for lip pursing
- Measure the respiratory rate (breaths per minute)
- Look around the patient for clues of disease, e.g. inhalers, nebuliser, sputum pot, oxygen cylinder/mask, peak expiratory flow rate (PEFR) diary.

INSPECTION

Hands

- Look for:
  finger clubbing
  signs of anaemia
  evidence of smoking
  peripheral cyanosis
- If finger clubbing is observed, examine the wrist for hypertrophic pulmonary osteoarthropathy (seen with advanced clubbing).

Respiratory causes of finger clubbing

Suppurative lung disease e.g. bronchiectasis, cystic fibrosis	Lung cancer	Alveolitis (fibrosing)	Mesothelioma

Test for tremor and CO_2 retention flap (asterixis)

- Ask the patient to put their arms straight out in front of them and fan their fingers apart. Look for a fine tremor (this may indicate use of a β_2 adrenoceptor agonist).
- Passively extend the wrists with the arms out-stretched. Involuntary flexion may represent a CO_2 retention flap.

Assess the radial pulse

(see Cardiovascular System Examination page 1)

Examine cervical and axillary lymph nodes

(see Lymph Nodes and Breast Examinations pages 84 & 88)

Assess the JVP

(see Cardiovascular System Examination page 3)

- This is raised in right ventricular failure due to pulmonary disease (cor pulmonale)

Features of Cor Pulmonale

- Raised JVP
- Hepatomegaly
- Right ventricular heave
- Peripheral/sacral oedema

Eye

- Look for:
  chemosis (oedema of the conjunctiva – may indicate CO_2 retention)
  anaemia (seen as pallor of the underside of the eyelid)
  ptosis (a drooping upper eyelid)
  miosis (constricted pupil) seen in Horner's syndrome associated with Pancoast's syndrome

Mouth

- Look under the tongue and at the lips for the blue tinge of central cyanosis
- Cyanosis is present if the deoxyhaemoglobin concentration is greater than 5 g/dl

EXAMINE THE PRAECORDIUM (CHEST)

- Look for:
  chest wall deformities (e.g. pectus excavatum/carinatum)
  scars anteriorly and posteriorly
- Inspect from the side to assess whether the chest is over-expanded (barrel chest)

PALPATION

- *Palpate the trachea to assess possible deviation. Gently place the index and middle fingers on either side of the trachea in the suprasternal notch.

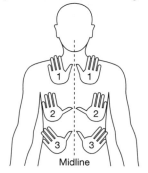

Palpation of the trachea (F: position of finger)

- Measure the crico-sternal distance: finger breadth distance between cricoid cartilage and suprasternal notch.
- Assess amount and symmetry of chest expansion by placing hands as in the diagram below (the thumbs must be off the chest and meet in the midline) and asking the patient to take deep breaths in and out. Note how far your thumbs separate with each inspiration. Assess expansion at the front and back.
- Palpate the left parasternal area for a right ventricular heave (felt in pulmonary hypertension), by placing your finger tips in the intercostal spaces just to the left of the sternum.
- Palpate the apex beat (may be difficult to feel with hyper-inflated lungs) and note its position.
- Test for tactile fremitus. Rest the ulnar aspect of the hand on the chest wall and ask the patient to say '99'. Note any abnormal vibrations. Do this at least six times – once in each of the hand positions illustrated on the diagram. Always compare left and right sides.

Position of hands for assessing chest expansion

---

* Warn the patient that this can be uncomfortable

PERCUSSION

- Spread out the fingers of one hand and rest the palm and fingers on the chest wall
- Position your middle finger in an intercostal space
- Strike the middle phalanx of this finger with the tip of the middle finger of the other hand. This technique needs lots of practice!
- Percuss the supraclavicular regions, the clavicles (tap each clavicle directly i.e. don't tap your finger), and the chest wall (in at least six positions to cover the entire lung fields). The axillae should not be missed.

✓ *Always compare left with right, by assessing both sides at each level.*

Characteristics of percussion notes

- Normal
- Hyper-resonant
- Dull
- Stony dull

- Move onto the back. Ask the patient to sit forward and fold their arms (to ensure the scapulae retract away from the area of percussion). Start just lateral to the vertebral column, and move laterally as you work down the back, as illustrated in the diagram below.

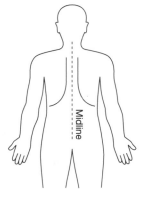

Midline

The curved lines indicate the "path" which should be taken during percussion and auscultation.

AUSCULTATION (with diaphragm of stethoscope)

- Auscultate the front and back by listening in the same positions in which you percussed, comparing sides at all times.
- Ask the patient to inspire deeply and then exhale (through their mouth) in each position of the stethoscope.
- Assess: whether breath sounds are vesicular (normal) or bronchial; the intensity of the breath sounds; and whether there are any adventitious (additional) breath sounds. If any abnormalities are heard, determine whether they occur on inspiration or expiration.

NB. If you want to experience the sound of auscultating bronchial breathing, listen over the trachea of a healthy individual.

Remember that patients may become dizzy if they are asked to deeply inspire and expire for prolonged periods.

Characteristics of breath sounds

- Intensity
- Pitch
- Ratio of inspiratory: expiratory phase
- Presence/absence of pause between inspiration and expiration
- Presence and timing of adventitious sounds: wheeze (rhonchi), crepitations (crackles)
- Other sounds: e.g. pleural rub

- Vocal fremitus can be assessed, by asking the patient to say '99' when you are auscultating. This is more reliable than tactile fremitus. It is not usually necessary to assess both tactile and vocal fremitus.

> ✓ *It is helpful to think of the anatomy of the lungs on percussion, palpation and auscultation to ensure that all lobes have been covered.*

Ensure that you ask to see any chest radiographs (*see Radiology chapter page 107 for interpretation of chest films*), lung function test results (spirometry and peak expiratory flow) and review any sputum pot contents.

It is important to distinguish between examining the alimentary system (mouth to anus) and the abdomen. At times you will be led to believe they are the same – they are not. The abdomen is a specific component of the alimentary system examination.

POSITIONING AND EXPOSURE

- Ask the patient to lie flat on the bed with their head on **one pillow** and to keep their arms straight by their side with palms facing upwards.
- You should expose the patient from nipple to knee although in practice exposure of only the abdomen is usual unless the groin is being closely examined).

INSPECTION

General

- Observe the patient and their surroundings from the end of the bed
- Observe for: abdominal movement with respiration, swelling, herniae, striae, cachexia, pallor, special diet or fluid charts on the bed, high energy drinks or drainage devices.

Hands

- Nails: leuconychia, clubbing
- Palms: palmar erythema, anaemia, Dupuytren's contracture
- Asterixis (liver flap): ask the patient to put their arms out straight in front with palms facing down and wrists cocked back. The eyes should be closed. Observe for a 'flapping' action of the wrist.

Face

- Eyes: sclera for jaundice (> 40 µg/l before clinically evident), anaemia (seen as pallor of the underside of the eyelid)
- Skin: jaundice, spider naevi

Mouth

- Observe for ulcers. Check tongue for dehydration or coating. Subtly smell the breath for hepatic foetor (smells like stale urine/ammonia), diabetic ketoacidosis (sweet/acetone smell) or halitosis.

Chest

- Check for: spider naevi (more than six is significant); gynaecomastia.

Abdomen

- Look closely for swellings, distended veins, skin changes (e.g. bruising), scars, herniae, pulsation, divarication of rectus muscles.
- Kneel down and look along the surface of the abdomen for peristaltic waves.
- Make a point of looking in the flanks e.g. for nephrectomy scars.

PALPATION

Features to palpate
- General
- Liver
- Spleen
- Kidneys
- Bladder
- Abdominal aorta

Before laying a finger on the patient's abdomen ask if there is any pain and, if so, leave the painful area until last (by which time, their confidence in you has developed).

If you know there is an area of pain, you may consider it useful to employ diversion/distraction tactics. Talk to the patient about something you know they enjoy or will be chatty about (e.g. hobbies, grandchildren, pets) and they may forget about any pain you may be inflicting.

General palpation

- Consists of **superficial and deep** palpation.
- For both – examine all nine regions of the abdomen in a systematic fashion (see diagram below).

> ✓ *Palpation should be performed whilst kneeling at the side of the bed so you are at the same level as the abdomen.*

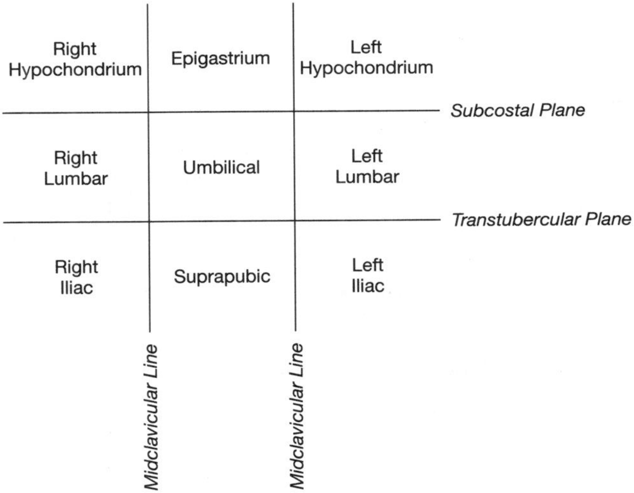

Right Hypochondrium	Epigastrium	Left Hypochondrium	
			Subcostal Plane
Right Lumbar	Umbilical	Left Lumbar	
			Transtubercular Plane
Right Iliac	Suprapubic	Left Iliac	

Midclavicular Line   *Midclavicular Line*

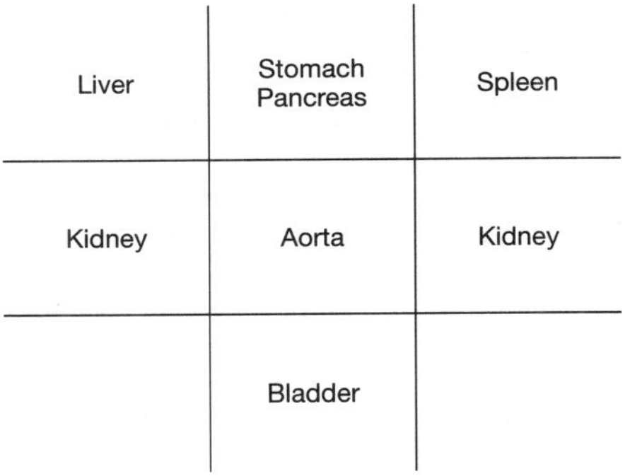

	Liver	Stomach Pancreas	Spleen
	Kidney	Aorta	Kidney
		Bladder	

Regions of the abdomen, and main organs found therein

✓ **You must watch the patient's face throughout palpation.**

Superficial palpation

With one hand flat on the abdomen, gently move the extended fingers up and down by flexing at the metacarpophalangeal (MCP joints). You are feeling for three features:

1. Tenderness (normal and rebound*)
2. Rigidity
3. Guarding

Deep palpation

This is usually performed with two hands (one on top of the other) and is used to detect masses and deep seated pain. Some doctors prefer you to use one hand only, and to push harder than for superficial palpation.

6 F's of the distended abdomen

- Fat
- Faeces
- Fluid
- Flatus
- Foetus (in females)
- Flipping great tumour

Liver

- For both the liver and spleen it is necessary to have respiration co-ordinated correctly with your palpation, since these organs move downward, below the costal margin, during inspiration (the lungs expand and the diaphragm moves inferiorly, thus pushing the liver inferiorly).
- To take advantage of this movement, use the expiratory phase to move your fingers into position and then hold them still during inspiration to try to feel the edge of these organs making contact with your fingers.

---

* Testing for rebound tenderness entails pushing the fingers in hard before quickly moving them away. Rebound tenderness is present if this procedure produces pain. If the patient is in noticeable pain, this technique is not necessary and light percussion alone may signify rebound tenderness (which reflects peritoneal involvement).

- For the liver, start in the right iliac fossa (RIF) and move superiorly to the costal margin.
- Many textbooks will recommend that the radial aspect of the index finger should be used, but it may be more effective to use the tips of the fingers of both hands. By doing this, a greater surface area will contact the liver, and a deeper push will be possible. However, short fingernails are a must!
- After the edge of the liver has been established, percuss the upper and lower borders of the liver to confirm your findings. The upper border is normally in the right 5th intercostal space.

You might ask: why examine the upper border of liver? As the capacity of the lungs increase, for example in emphysema, the liver is pushed inferiorly giving a false sense of liver enlargement (pseudo-hepatomegaly).

Liver features to be palpated

- Size
- Surface (micro- or macro-nodular)
- Edge (e.g. smooth, nobbly)
- Pulsation

✓ *Enlargement of the liver/spleen should be recorded in centimetres (not finger breadths).*

Spleen

The examination of the spleen follows a similar format to the liver.

Start in the right iliac fossa (RIF), but this time work up to the left hypochondrium (since the spleen enlarges diagonally). The lateral tilt may then be performed. Ask the patient to turn slightly onto their right side and examine the spleen again.

✓ *With your non-examining hand you should splint the left lower rib from behind, to fix the spleen, making it more easily palpable anteriorly.*

Differentiating a splenic from a renal mass

- Spleen has a notched edge
- You cannot get 'above' the spleen
- Spleen descends towards the right iliac fossa on inspiration
- Spleen is not ballotable
- Spleen is dull to percussion

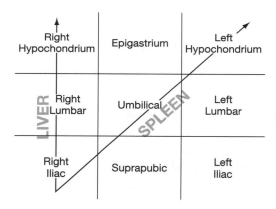

'Paths' taken in palpation of the liver and spleen

Kidneys

- The kidneys are bimanually palpated. Some call this ballotment, although this is not strictly true as this term refers to the movement of a solid within a fluid medium (like dunking an apple in a bowl of water).
- One hand should be placed on the abdomen, and should remain **fixed**; the other hand is placed posteriorly, and is used to 'flick' or 'bounce' the kidney between your hands (hence bimanual!).

Bladder

- To palpate the bladder use the ulnar aspect of the hand and gently press over the suprapubic space – this is usually where an enlarged bladder will lie.

- An enlarged bladder can be confirmed with light percussion. The dullness will extend to the pubic rim.

Abdominal aorta

- You should place your fingers just above the umbilicus and push down firmly (but not too hard). The index and middle finger should be held together as one unit. An abdominal aneurysm will usually make your fingers move upwards (pulsatile movement) and outwards (expansile movement).
- The abdominal aorta may be palpated in some normal individuals and will feel pulsatile (try on a thin friend).

NB. If you suspect that the patient may have an abdominal tumour take time to palpate the supraclavicular nodes, especially on the left hand side. This is because tumours may spread along the lymphatic duct to this location (TROISIER'S NODE).

PERCUSSION

Percussion should be carried out only when necessary – for example, with a suspected swollen abdomen.

Shifting dullness

- Percuss with the same technique as for the respiratory examination with a flat middle finger of the left hand placed on the abdomen and the middle finger of the right hand used as your 'hammer'. The action should be a flicking one with movement chiefly at the wrist not a stabbing movement with a stiff wrist. The left hand should be orientated with the fingers pointed towards the patient's head.
- Start at the umbilicus, and percuss across the abdomen laterally until you find any change in the sound. It is likely to go from resonant to dull. This change signifies an interface between air (resonant) and fluid (dull). The reason it is resonant in the centre of the abdomen is that air is present within loops of bowel causing them to float on any fluid. Fluid goes to the flanks as gravity dictates.
- Mark the border at which you found the change in sound before asking the patient to roll towards you on to their right hand side.

- Percuss again and re-establish the area where the change from resonant to dull occurs. If fluid is present, the border will have changed as all the fluid from the left moves making the area resonant. The dullness has shifted.

Fluid thrill

- Ask the patient to put the ulnar edge of one of their hands in the centre of the abdomen, orientated in a head-to-toe direction (this is done to prevent the movement of fat that may feel like a thrill).
- Now flick the abdomen on one side, while keeping your other hand on the other side to feel any movement transmitted across – if you feel a thrill, it is due to movement through the fluid.
- To understand this concept, fill a balloon half full with water and tap one side whilst feeling the other side. You can feel the ripple of the water and, unlike in the abdomen, you can see it too!

AUSCULTATION

This is done to hear bowel sounds, of which there are four types:

Types of bowel sounds

- Normal
- Borborygmi (with increased peristalsis)
- Absent (with ileus)
- Tinkling (with obstruction)

Use the diaphragm of the stethoscope and keep it in position (over the centre of the abdomen) for a minimum of 15 seconds.

You must also auscultate in at least three places to test for bruits:

1. Abdominal aorta
2. Kidneys (for renovascular disease)*
3. Liver

---

* Auscultate just above the umbilicus 2 cm from the midline.

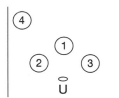

Positions for auscultation for bruits:
U = umbilicus; 1 = abdominal aorta;
2 & 3 = renovascular; 4 = liver

✓ **All alimentary examinations must end by undertaking an examination of the groin (including inguinal lymph nodes), rectum and genitalia.**

There are many more special tests which can be performed if specific pathology is suspected. (*See Radiology chapter page 115 for interpretation of a plain abdominal radiograph.*)

OVERVIEW

No clinical speciality has as many examinations or special tests as those in musculoskeletal medicine. In fact sometimes there is often more than one way of examining the same thing!

Initially this may daze, bewilder and erode self-confidence but once you establish a routine and practise your technique, all examinations can be done quickly and efficiently.

Common musculoskeletal examinations

- GALS Screen
- Spine
- Upper limb: shoulder, hand and wrist
- Lower limb: hip, knee, ankle and foot

All these examinations follow the same overall format.

Examination format

- Look (inspection)
- Feel (palpation)
- Measure
- Movements
- Special Tests

Measurements (if applicable) and special tests can come wherever you choose in the general routine of the examination, and should be done at the most convenient moment for both yourself and the patient. As long as you have a smooth memorable system, it does not matter about the order. For example, although it is perfectly feasible to measure the true and apparent lengths of the leg at the end of the hip examination, we recommend that it is done after palpation. This is because you will have identified an important landmark, the anterior superior iliac spine (ASIS), and so you are less likely to forget this aspect of the examination.

Make sure you inspect any appropriate radiographs.

THE GALS SCREEN

This general musculoskeletal screening test covers the basics of many of the more detailed examinations given later. It is essentially a primary care and non-specialist test to filter out those who need specialist referral.

The Gait, Arms, Legs, Spine test can be comfortably performed in five minutes, and should follow the format: three questions, Gait, Spine, Arms, Legs for practical purposes. You should look for, and record, any abnormalities in any aspect of the screening test.

Questions

- Have you any pain or stiffness in your muscles, joints or back?
- Can you dress yourself completely without any difficulty?
- Can you walk up and down stairs without any difficulty?

GAIT

- Ask the patient to walk to the other side of the room, turn, and walk back to you

SPINE

- Inspect the patient standing from in front, the side and behind
- Ask the patient to bend over and touch their toes, keeping the knees straight (lumbar flexion)
- You can estimate the amount of flexion by putting fingers on adjacent lumbar vertebrae and noting the distance that they separate during flexion.
- Ask the patient to put 'their ear on their shoulder' on each side in turn (lateral cervical flexion).
- Squeeze the supraspinatus muscles, whose positions are shown in the diagram opposite.

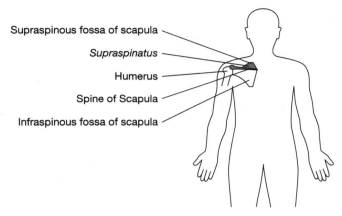

Supraspinous fossa of scapula

Supraspinatus

Humerus

Spine of Scapula

Infraspinous fossa of scapula

Location of the supraspinatus muscle

ARMS

- Inspect the patient's arms extended by their side in the anatomical position, as shown in the diagram.

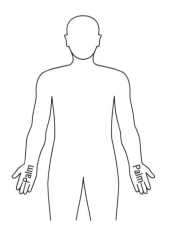

- Keeping their elbows by their side (so fixing them) flex the elbow to 90° and ask the patient to turn their palms towards the ceiling, then down to the floor (supination and pronation).
- Squeeze across the 2ND–5TH MCP joints, and note any pain.
- Ask the patient to touch with their thumb each finger in turn.
- Ask the patient to make a fist
- Ask the patient to put their hands behind their head and to bring their elbows backwards.

The position of the arms for inspection

LEGS

With the patient standing

- Inspect when standing – from the front, side and from behind (pay special attention to the popliteal fossa).

With the patient on the couch

- Inspect the legs close up
- Feel the temperature of the knee by placing the back of your hand over the anterior aspect.
- Carry out the bulge test (+/- the patellar tap) for a fluid effusion in the knee (*see Knee Examination page 46*).
- Ask the patient to put their heel up to their bottom (active knee and hip flexion)
- Passively flex the hip
- Whilst the hip is still flexed, test internal rotation passively (*see Hip Examination page 39*).
- Extend the knee, keeping one hand over the patella to feel for crepitus.
- Squeeze across the 2nd–5th metatarsophalangeal (MTP) joints.
- Inspect the foot closely for callosities and other abnormalities. Look between the toes, at the metatarsal heads and the heel.

SPINE

The spine is essentially composed of three components to examine: the cervical, thoracic and lumbar spine. There are occasions when examination may be required on only one component of the spine.

INSPECTION

- It may be immediately obvious to you as a patient enters the room that their spine is abnormal. Look at the way they walk, the posture they take, how they hold their neck and the manner in which they sit.

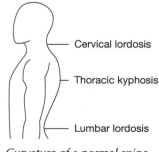

Cervical lordosis

Thoracic kyphosis

Lumbar lordosis

Curvature of a normal spine

- The patient should be adequately exposed (i.e. without a shirt/blouse) to observe properly, since clothes may hide subtle signs.
- Inspect the patient sitting and standing from behind, in front and the side.
- Abnormal kyphosis, lordosis (increased or absent) or scoliosis (a deviation from the midline) should be noted.
- Ask the patient to stand with his/her back against the wall. Normally you should see the following in contact with the wall: occiput, shoulders, buttocks, heels. If not, an abnormality is present.

PALPATION

Feel for the following bony landmarks:

- Vertebra prominens at C7-T1 junction
- Spinous processes from C6 inferiorly to sacrum
- Facet joints (that lie 1 cm lateral to spinous processes)
- Sacroiliac joints (beneath Dimples of Venus at S2)
- Palpate the paraspinal muscles (abnormal curvature can be due to muscle spasm).

MEASURE

Schober's Test

- Identify the Dimples of Venus
- Use a tape measure and mark (with water soluble ink) a point 10 cm superior to the Dimples, and 5 cm inferior, in the midline (as shown in the diagram).
- Ask the patient to flex the lumbar spine (i.e. touch their toes)
- The distance between the two marks should be measured when the patient's spine is flexed maximally.
- The distance should increase to more than 21 cm if normal.

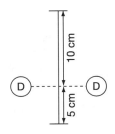

Landmark's for Schober's Test (D = Dimple of Venus)

Rib excursion

- Measure the chest diameter with the patient in full expiration and full inspiration; note the difference between the two.

MOVEMENTS

All movements of the spine are tested actively, since passive movements are not feasible.

Cervical

- Flexion (look down at toes)
- Extension (look up at ceiling)
- Lateral flexion (put your ear onto each shoulder in turn)
- Lateral rotation (look over each shoulder in turn)

When assessing lateral flexion and rotation, you may wish to hold the shoulders to ensure that the cervical spine moves and not the shoulders.

Thoracic and lumbar

- Flexion (touch your toes)
- Extension (lean backwards)
- Lateral flexion (slide your hand down the side of your leg on both left and right sides)
- Lateral rotation (twist at the waist, to both left and right)

✓ *When assessing lateral rotation, it is important to fix the pelvis. Do this by stabilising the pelvis with your hands, or by performing the examination with the patient seated.*

SPECIAL TESTS

Straight leg raising test (for nerve root irritation):

- With the patient supine, the examiner uses his arm to fix the pelvis across the ASIS. The patient attempts to flex the hip with the knee fully extended (i.e. raise a straight leg towards the ceiling).

Stretch Test (for sciatic nerve root irritation)

● With the limit of straight leg raising reached, allow the leg to lower slightly, then dorsiflex the foot (push the toes towards the head) quickly. If this causes severe pain the test is positive. Flexing the knee may relieve the pain.

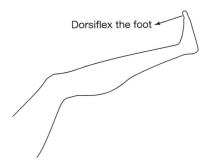

Dorsiflex the foot

Stretch Test

A neurological examination is advisable in conjunction with an examination of the spine due to their anatomical relationship.

SHOULDER

The shoulder, unlike some other major joints, is made up of multiple parts that cannot be tested in isolation. It is a shallow joint making it susceptible to injury both of the joint itself and the surrounding soft tissue structures. The capsule and rotator cuff muscles (supraspinatus, infraspinatus, teres minor, subscapularis) stabilise the shoulder joint.

Joints at the shoulder girdle

● Glenohumeral
● Acromioclavicular
● Sternoclavicular
● Thoracoscapular

Sources of shoulder pain

- Shoulder joint
- Axilla
- Cervical spine
- Sub-diaphragmatic
- Cardiac

INSPECTION

- Ask the patient to expose their top half for a proper examination. Watching the patient undress may allow assessment of functional impairment resulting from shoulder pathology.
- Inspect from: in front, the side and behind (with the patient standing).
- Observe for: asymmetry, muscle wasting (especially of the deltoid), abnormal posture, swelling, scars, bruising, deformity, level of the shoulders (are they level?). Also inspect the axillae.

✓ *Ask if the shoulder is painful before examination.*

PALPATION (for joint anatomy)

- Stand in front of the patient, face to face
- Palpate the following structures, in this order:
  sternoclavicular joint
  clavicle
  acromioclavicular joint
  acromial process
  head of humerus
  coracoid process
  spine of scapula (from behind)
  greater tuberosity of humerus
- Observe the patient's face for any tenderness and feel for swelling and crepitus.

✓ *Use the dorsum of your hand to feel the temperature over the shoulder.*

MEASURE

- Assess the deltoid bulk by measuring the circumference at the top of both arms.

MOVEMENTS

Shoulder movements

- Flexion
- Extension
- Abduction
- Adduction
- Internal Rotation
- External Rotation

- Movements should be tested actively by asking the patient to perform the movements shown in the following diagrams.
- Stand with the patient face to face with you, and ask them to copy the movements you make.

Flexion: flex the elbow to 90°, move the arm upward until the fist points backward.

Extension: flex the elbow to 90°, move the arm backward as far as possible.

Abduction: with the elbow fully extended, bring the arm away from the body until the fingertips point to the ceiling.

Adduction: with the elbow fully extended, bring the arm across the trunk.

External and internal rotation: with the elbow fixed to 90°, pinned into the side, move the forearm in an arc-like motion, thus separating the hands (external rotation), and bringing them together (internal rotation).

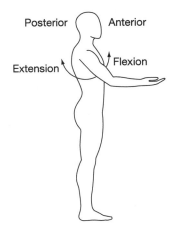

Flexion and extension of the shoulder

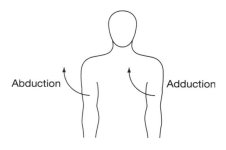

Abduction and adduction of the shoulder

• When testing internal/external rotation it is important for the elbow to be fixed by the side to ensure the movement occurs at the shoulder girdle.

• The elbows should be flexed to 90°.

✓ **You should use one hand to fix the scapula during abduction and adduction so that you can take into account any movement here. Movement of the scapula can give the false impression of movement at the shoulder.**

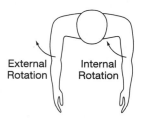

Internal and external rotation of the shoulder (viewed from above)

• You may wish, in addition, to test functional movement of the shoulder by asking the patient to:

1. Put their hands behind their head with the elbows as far back as possible.
2. Scratch the centre of the back as far up as possible.

• You should next test the movements passively. Ask the patient to relax, and move the arm so as to test all movements at the shoulder.

SPECIAL TESTS

• Serratus anterior: ask the patient to push against the wall with flat palms; observe the scapulae for winging (caused by muscle weakness).

• Ask the patient to abduct the shoulder against the force of your hands (painful in supraspinatus tendonitis).

- Ask the patient to shrug their shoulder against the force of your hands (difficult in pathology of cranial nerve XI).
- Test the sensation over the 'Regimental Badge Area' on the skin over the deltoid muscle (to assess axillary nerve sensory function).
- Test the circulation to the upper limb (as an injury at the shoulder can compromise the blood supply) – palpate the brachial and radial arteries.

HAND AND WRIST

Anatomically and functionally the hand is a complex structure. There is much more to examination of the hand than examining the joints. Diseases of wide variation may manifest in the hands, but are easily missed if a systematic approach is not used and too much attention is paid to the multitude of joints.

The examination of the hand begins as soon as you meet the patient – when you shake hands. A tremor, painful joints, warmth, weakness or lack of digits are just a few points you may note.

For those specifically trying to identify major hand pathology, the patient should be asked to identify their dominant hand as this may have functional implications.

INSPECTION

✓ *The hands should be placed on a white pillow.*

- Look at the dorsal and palmar surfaces.
  Observe for: scars, hand posture, skin changes, deformities, subluxation, muscle wasting (especially at thenar/hypothenar eminences), swelling (bony, soft or fluid), palmar erythema, sweatiness, tremor, evidence of smoking.
- Look closely at the nails.
  Observe for: pitting, hyperkeratosis, leuconychia, koilonychia, onycholysis, ridging, Beau's lines, micro-infarcts, dilated capillary loops, discoloration.

- Try to identify any deformities. Note the pattern of joint deformity as this may be important diagnostically.
- Assess tremor by placing a sheet of paper on top of the patient's hands when the arms are outstretched.

Deformities of the hands and wrists

- Ulnar deviation at the wrists/MCP joints
- Subluxation of the wrist/MCP joints
- Prominence of the ulnar styloid
- Heberden's distal interphalangeal joint (DIP) or Bouchard's proximal interphalangeal joint (PIP) nodes of osteoarthritis (OA)
- Squaring of the hand at the thumb carpometacarpal joints (in OA)
- Rheumatoid deformities: boutonniere (PIPs), swan neck, z-shaped thumb
- Gouty tophi or finger pulp calcinosis
- Fixed flexion contracture of digit
- Dupuytren's contracture (usually the little and ring fingers)

PALPATION

- Gently palpate around the wrist and all the small joints of the hand: carpal bones, carpometacarpal (CMC), MCP, PIP and DIP joints.

✓ *Pay special attention to palpation in the anatomical snuffbox, since scaphoid pathology is easily missed.*

- Be aware of: swelling, tenderness, bony abnormalities, temperature, crepitus.
- Squeeze across the MCP joints and ask about tenderness.

MOVEMENTS

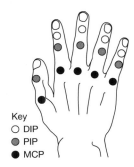

Key
○ DIP
◔ PIP
● MCP

Joints in the hand: PIP, DIP, MCP, interphalangeal.

Before testing hand movements check the patient has good shoulder function, as without it hand function is limited. To do this, ask the patient to place their hands behind their heads, with elbows well back.

Wrist

- Pronation and supination: the patient's elbows must be fixed and held pinned into the side. Ask the patient to turn their palms towards the floor (pronation), and then towards the sky (supination) Remember: supinate to the sky!

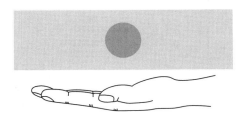

Supinate to the sky!

- Flexion and dorsi-flexion (extension): ask the patient to form the prayer (dorsi-flexion) and inverse prayer (flexion) positions. For the inverse prayer position put the dorsal (back of hand) surfaces of the hands together.

The prayer position

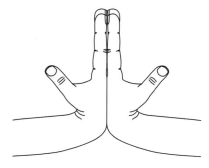

The inverse prayer position

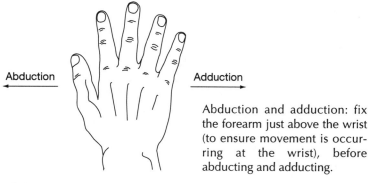

Abduction

Adduction

Abduction and adduction: fix the forearm just above the wrist (to ensure movement is occurring at the wrist), before abducting and adducting.

Abduction and adduction of the wrist

Digits

- Thumb: extension, flexion, abduction, adduction and opposition. These can all be done in seconds with the patient's dorsal surface flat on the pillow whilst the examiner fixes the wrist to prevent interference.

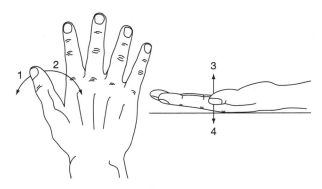

Some thumb movements: 1 = extension; 2 = flexion; 3 = abduction; 4 = adduction

- Fingers (flexion and extension): ask the patient to make a fist and to open it out.
- Abduction and adduction: ask the patient to keep hands parallel to the ground and spread their fingers apart and back together.
- Grips: ask the patient to squeeze your finger tightly inside their clenched fist. You may also wish to test: precision grip (roll a coin between finger and thumb); ball grip (pick up a tennis ball); flat pinch (hold a key between forefinger and thumb); writing (hold a pen); hook (carry a suitcase); unscrewing (unscrew the lid of a jar).

✓ If it is apparent that a patient has limited movement in the hand joints, do not persevere trying to get them to perform movements again and again. It is very distressing to have limited hand function as it reduces one's ability to carry out activities of daily living.

SPECIAL TESTS (for carpal tunnel syndrome)

- Tinel's Test: percuss for 30 seconds over the carpal tunnel on the flexor aspect of the wrist to try to elicit the symptoms of carpal tunnel syndrome.

- Phalen's Test: hold the hands in the inverse prayer position for a minute to try to elicit symptoms.

NB. Many more tests exist for individual tendons and muscles. These are very much the territory of specialists. A mastery of the above will stand you in good stead as a generalist.

NEUROVASCULAR STATE

There are three nerves which supply motor and sensory function to the hands: the median, radial and ulnar nerves.

Motor function

- Radial: ask the patient to fully flex the wrists (see above, inverse prayer position).
- Ulnar: with the patient's fingers fully adducted slide a piece of paper between the ring and middle finger. Ask the patient to try to stop you pulling the paper away. Alternatively you may test for Froment's sign. To do this, ask the patient to hold a piece of paper/card between the thumbs and the radial aspect of the index finger. Then pull the paper away and ask the patient to stop it. The test is abnormal if either of the thumbs flex at the IP joint.

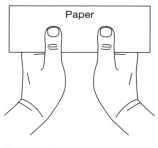

Froment's sign

- Median: ask the patient to oppose the thumb and index finger and stop you (the examiner) from breaking the circle which this forms.

Sensory function

- Ask the patient to close their eyes for all these tests to eliminate bias. Test pinprick and fine touch (*see Peripheral Neurological Examination page 59*).
- Radial: touch in the anatomical snuffbox.
- Ulnar: touch over the medial one and a half fingers on the palm (little finger, and medial half of ring finger)

- Median: touch over the lateral three and a half fingers on the palm (lateral half of ring finger, index finger and thumb).

Palpate the radial and ulnar pulses. You may also wish to perform Allen's Test for perfusion of the hand.

Allen's Test
- Ask the patient to make a fist
- Occlude both the radial and ulnar arteries by pressing over them
- Press for five seconds
- Ask the patient to open the palm whilst you release the pressure on each artery in turn and watch the colour of the palm; it should change from pale to pink as blood flow is re-established

---

HIP

INSPECTION

With the patient standing

- Expose the leg by asking the patient to undress down to their underwear.
- Observe from all sides with the patient standing stationary. When inspecting from behind, look specifically at the level of the iliac crests and for the presence of a raised gluteal fold.
- Ask the patient to walk to the other side of the room, turn round and walk back. Observe carefully for the use of a walking aid, an abnormal gait pattern or stride length, and also for evidence of pain.

With the patient on the couch

- The angle of the bed should be 45°
- You require full exposure of the pelvic region to inspect properly. You should look at both sides from in front and behind (i.e. the buttocks).

PALPATION

Feel for the major landmarks:

- ASIS
- Ischial spine

In some circumstances it may be necessary to palpate for temperature and tenderness of the hip joint, but as it is a deep seated joint, this is rarely of any value.

MEASURE

Use a measuring tape to measure:

- Apparent Length: xiphisternum to medial malleolus
- True Length: ASIS to medial malleolus

> ✓ *Some will advise that the umbilicus should be used as a landmark for measurement rather than the xiphisternum. The latter should be used since it is a fixed point.*

Inequality of leg length of more than 2 cm between sides causes joint overload.

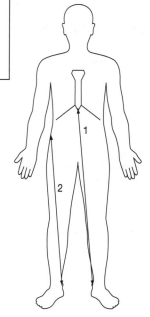

*Measuring leg length
(1=apparent length; 2=true length)*

MOVEMENTS

All six movements that take place at the hip must be examined both ACTIVELY and PASSIVELY. These movements are:

Hip movements

- Flexion
- Extension

- Abduction
- Adduction

- Internal rotation
- External rotation

Movements should be examined in this order, except for extension which is done last since it requires the patient to lie prone (on their tummy).

The pelvis needs to be fixed for most movements of the hip in order that the movement observed is due to movement of the hip joint and not the pelvis (tilt and shift). The pelvis is fixed by using your left hand to stabilise the contralateral ASIS.

Active movements are performed by asking the patient to perform the following movements:

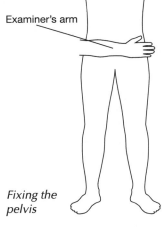

Examiner's arm

Fixing the pelvis

- Flexion: ask patient to bring the heel up to their bottom
- Abduction: move a straight leg away from the midline
- Adduction: move a straight leg across the midline
- Internal rotation: ask the patient to lie prone, to keep the knees together and to separate the ankles as far as possible

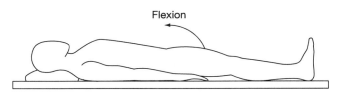

Flexion

Hip flexion

- External rotation: ask the patient to lie prone and to cross the feet over one another
- Extension: ask the patient to lie prone and to raise their leg off the bed

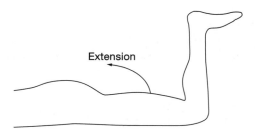

Hip extension

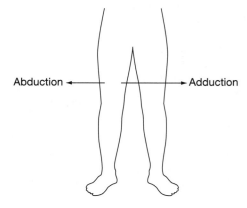

Hip abduction and adduction

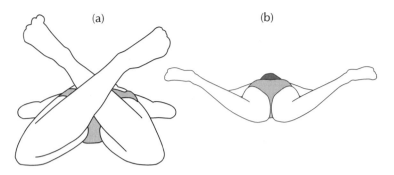

Active hip external (a) and internal (b) rotation

Passive movements are performed by asking the patient to relax, while you (the examiner) move the limb.

- Flex hip: move the heel up towards the bottom (as with active) and then push knee towards the patient's body.
- Abduct hip: as for active, but done by examiner with the patient relaxed.
- Adduct hip: as for active, but done by examiner with patient relaxed.
- Internally rotate hip: flex the knee and stabilise it with one hand. With the other hand, move the heel laterally. The heel moves away from the midline, but the knee, and hip, rotate internally (i.e. towards the midline).
- Externally rotate hip: flex the knee and stabilise it with one hand. With the other hand, move the heel medially. The heel moves towards the midline, but the knee and hip rotate externally (i.e. away from the midline).
- Extend hip: with the patient **prone**, lift the thigh up off the bed by pulling the foot directly upwards with the knee flexed to 90°.

Internal and external rotation can also be tested with the hip extended. With the patient lying prone, flex the knee to 90°, and then move the feet to separate them (internal rotation) and to cross them over (external rotation).

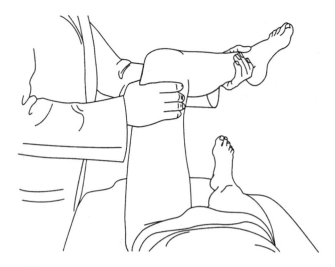

Passive hip external rotation

SPECIAL TESTS

There are two main special tests in the hip examination:

- Trendelenburg Test (for hip stability)
- Thomas' Test (for fixed flexion deformities)

Trendelenburg Test

Observe the patient from behind

- Ask the patient to support their weight on the right hip only (i.e. ask them to lift their left leg off the ground by bending the knee).
- Watch the pelvis, and note the direction of tilt
- In normal individuals, the pelvis will rise on the side of the leg that has been lifted
- With instability, the pelvis may drop on the side of the leg that has been lifted
- Repeat the test with the patient standing on the other leg

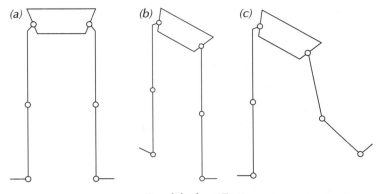

Trendelenburg Test

a   Standing on both legs
b   Normal – the pelvis rises on the side of the lifted leg
c   Abnormal – the pelvis drops on the side of the lifted leg

Thomas' Test

- Put your left hand (palm upwards) beneath the lumbar spine to ensure that it remains flattened during the test.
- With the other hand, passively flex one hip
- While you are flexing this hip, observe the movement of the other leg – in the event of a fixed flexion deformity (common in hip OA) the opposite leg flexes too.
- Repeat the test on the other hip

✓ *Hip pathology may present with knee pain as they share obturator and femoral nerve supply. For this reason, the hip should always be examined in patients presenting with knee pain.*

KNEE

A full examination of the knee can be very time consuming. The complete process is described here, but be prepared to carry out a modification of this as circumstances dictate.

✓ *Remember that you should examine both knees, even when only one appears to be abnormal.*

INSPECTION

With the patient standing

- Inspect the knees from in front, the side and behind whilst the patient is standing stationary. In particular, note the presence or absence of a varus or valgus deformity.
- Inspect the patient's gait as they walk to the other side of the room, turn and come back.

With the patient on the couch

- Inspect the knees close up whilst on the bed. Look for fine details such as scars, small volumes of fluid, cysts and muscle state.
- Ask the patient to bend the knee, and note the presence of tibial sag (seen with posterior cruciate ligament damage).

PALPATION

- Temperature: use the dorsum of your hand to feel the temperature over the knee (compare sides).
- The quadriceps tendon, patella and patellar ligament should be palpated for abnormal anatomy.
- Now palpate the joint line. You may wish to ask the patient to slightly bend the knee whilst doing this to confirm the location of the joint line.
- Palpate the patello-femoral joint, including beneath the patella.
- Palpate the popliteal fossa, chiefly to detect for the presence of a popliteal aneurysm or a cyst.
- Palpate for fluid effusions either using the bulge test (little fluid) or the patellar tap test (for a larger volume of fluid).

PERFORMING FLUID TESTS

Bulge Test

Using your index and middle fingers together as a unit sweep along the medial aspect of the knee, thus forcing any fluid to the lateral side (1). Then sweep along the lateral side of the knee (2) and watch to see if a bulge occurs on the medial side as the fluid moves back .

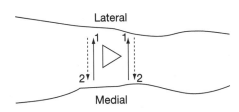

Bulge test (see text for explanation of numbers)

Patella Tap Test

Using the curve formed between the extended thumb and the index finger, milk down any fluid from above the knee. Using the index and middle fingers of the other hand, push (not tap) the patella down firmly. If fluid is present, the patella will bounce off the lateral femoral condyle behind. You will feel this as a tap – hence the name of the test.

MEASURE

Using a tape measure, obtain the circumference (in centimetres) of both legs around the bulk of the quadriceps muscles. Measure from a fixed bony point so that a comparable reading is taken for both sides.

MOVEMENTS

Movement should be tested actively, then passively. Flexion and extension are the main movements at this joint. You may also wish to examine for hyperextension (recurvatum).

- Flexion: ask the patient to bend their leg at the knee
- Extension: ask the patient to straighten their leg
- Hyperextension: lift the leg off the bed and gently push the knee downward from above to see if it will extend any further

Assess flexion and extension passively by asking the patient to relax while you (the examiner) perform the movements. Place your hand over the patella when you are testing passive movement, and note the presence or absence of crepitus.

SPECIAL TESTS

There a quite a few special tests for the knee and all can be performed conveniently at the end of the examination. The knee is very much dependent on soft tissues for stability and range of function. These tests aim to assess their integrity.

Testing the lateral/medial collateral ligaments

If this test is carried out in 30° of flexion it tests the collateral ligaments alone. If performed with the knee extended, it also tests the posterior capsule and is thus not specific to the collateral ligament.

- The knee should be flexed to 30°
- Support the medial aspect of the thigh, and push medially on the lateral aspect of the lower leg (shown in italics on the diagram opposite). This tests the lateral collateral ligament.
- Then, support the lateral aspect of the thigh, and push laterally on the medial aspect of the lower leg (shown in capitals on the diagram opposite). This tests the medial collateral ligament.
- Excessive movement may indicate ligament damage

Side view: bend the leg to 30° of flexion

Testing the anterior/posterior cruciate ligaments

The integrity of these ligaments may be assessed using the anterior and posterior drawer tests (which are performed at the same time). With both tests it is essential that the patient is relaxed.

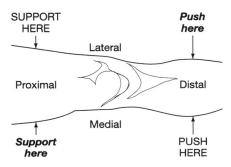

Top view: testing the integrity of the ligaments

With the patient supine on the couch, ask them to flex their knee to about 90°. Palpate the bulk of the quadriceps muscles to ensure that the patient is relaxed.

After checking that there is no pain in the foot, perch yourself (one buttock) on the foot to stabilise the lower leg. With both hands wrap the fingers around the back of the knee, keeping the thumbs in front over the patella. Position the thumbs so they point directly towards the ceiling. Pull the leg forward (to test anterior cruciate) and push backwards (to test posterior cruciate). Excessive movement may indicate ligament damage.

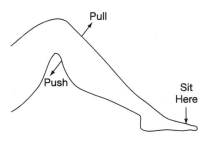

Position of leg for testing the cruciate ligaments. Pulling tests the anterior ligament; pushing tests the posterior ligament.

Testing the Menisci

Apley's grinding test can be used for this purpose.

- With the patient prone ('please turn onto your tummy'), flex the knee to 90°.
- Use your left hand to stabilise the lower leg behind the knee and with the right hand, grip the heel of the foot.

- Twist the foot in a 'grinding motion' as shown in the diagram. This test may cause pain if a meniscus is damaged.

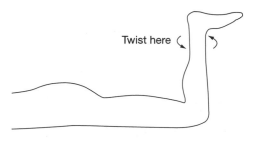

Apley's grinding test

NEUROVASCULAR STATE

The peripheral pulses (popliteal, posterior tibial, dorsalis pedis) and sensation below the knee should be undertaken to finish. For sensation, fine touch and proprioception are tested routinely. Other senses may be tested if this is a primary problem. (*See Cardiovascular and Peripheral Nervous System Examinations pages 1 & 59.*)

In theory, all joint examinations should involve the adjacent joints being examined. In reality this is not always the case but the knee is an important source of referred hip pain, especially in children. This is because the knee and hip share a partially similar nerve supply.

✓ *Therefore, all knee examinations should be accompanied by a hip examination. If time limitations do not permit this, you should state that it would be your intention to examine the hip as well.*

ANKLE AND FOOT

The ankle frequently requires examination, given its potential for injury and the weight borne by this joint in the course of everyday activities. However, it is not a simple joint, either anatomically or functionally, so a systematic approach is required.

INSPECTION

With the patient standing

- **Gait**: observe the patient's gait as they walk across to the other side of the room, turn around, and walk back with shoes on.

The legs and feet should then be clearly exposed before continuing with the examination.

- **Appearance**: look for swelling, muscle wasting or deformity on any aspect of the foot.
- **Posture**: when standing with the foot flat and on tip-toes
- **Arches**: longitudinal (medial/lateral) and transverse (under metatarsal heads). Note any pes cavus (high arched foot) or pes planus (flat foot).

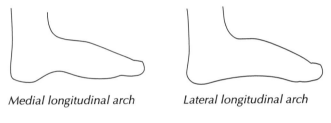

Medial longitudinal arch   *Lateral longitudinal arch*

          Transverse arch (foot sectioned in a coronal plane)

- **Gait**: observe the patient's gait as they walk across to the other side of the room, turn around, and walk back. Note if the patient walks on the border of the foot. Gait should also be examined with the patient walking on tip-toes.
- **Footwear**: be attentive to the nature of the footwear and how the shoe has worn. The back of the shoe may reveal wear suggestive of abnormal loading.

With the patient on the couch

- **Heel and sole**: look for callosities (signifies abnormal loading) and ulcers.
- **Toe nails**: look for any abnormalities (e.g. in-growing toenail, trophic changes)

- **Toes**: mallet toe, hammer toe (usually 2nd toe), bunion (1st metatarsal joint), bunionette (5th metatarsal joint) or clawing of the toes. Look between toes for ulcers and other abnormalities.

PALPATION

- **Temperature**: feel over the main joints with the dorsum of your hand

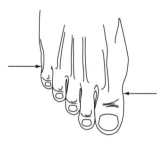

Squeezing across the MTP joints

- **Bony prominences**: lateral/medial malleoli, metatarsophalangeal (MTP) joints, interphalangeal (IP) joints and heel. Squeeze across metatarsal joints 1–5 (as shown in the diagram), and note any pain.
- **Achilles tendon**: is a gap palpable between the ends of a ruptured tendon
- Any abnormalities on the foot e.g. lumps or swellings
- Finally, press deep into the sole of the foot (for spurs)

MEASURE

It may be helpful to measure the 'calf girth' on the right and left side, in order to obtain an objective measure of any muscle wasting or hypertrophy.

MOVEMENTS

Movements take place at the ankle joint, sub-talar joint, mid-tarsal joint, MTP and IP joints. Active and passive movements should be assessed where possible. These can be performed with the patient sitting on the couch with their legs hanging over the edge (knees flexed and lower leg relaxed). The following movements should be tested:

- Dorsiflexion (point the toes towards the head) and plantar flexion (point the toes towards the floor). Fix the heel to ensure that these movements occur at the ankle joint.

- Inversion (turn the sole in towards the midline) and eversion (turn the sole away from the midline). In order to maintain a neutral position, hold the heel when testing these movements. These movements occur at the sub-tarsal and mid-tarsal joints.
- Flexion (curl the toes) and extension (straighten the toes)
- Abduction (fan the toes) and adduction of toes (try to hold a piece of paper between the toes).

SPECIAL TESTS

Simmond's (squeeze) Test (tests for rupture of the Achilles tendon). Ask the patient to kneel on a chair with their feet hanging over the edge, holding the back of the chair for stability. Squeeze the gastrocnemius muscle gently. Normally the foot will plantar-flex; if the Achilles tendon is ruptured, no plantar flexion will occur.

NEUROVASCULAR STATE

Palpate the dorsalis pedis and posterior tibial pulses (*see Cardiovascular System page 1*).

Assess fine touch, pin prick, proprioception, vibration and temperature sensation. Routinely, assessment of vibration sense and proprioception is sufficient (*see Peripheral Nervous System page 59*).

CRANIAL NERVES

Full examination of the cranial nerves is quite a complex process, requiring many separate tests to be carried out. It is therefore especially important that a system of examination should be learnt for easy recall. A good way of remembering the examination is to work your way through each nerve in turn, and assess sensory and motor function where appropriate. This is an examination of applied anatomy.

OLFACTORY – I

- Usually sufficient to ask if the patient has noticed a problem with smelling or tasting food
- Formal testing requires using an aromatic material (such as orange peel or coffee granules) to test the patient's perception and identification
- Test both nostrils separately

OPTIC – II *(see Eye Examination page 76)*

- Inspect the eye and note pupil size, shape and equality between sides
- Assess direct and consensual pupil reactions to light and accommodation
- Test visual acuity
- Test colour vision
- Test visual fields by confrontation
- Examine the fundus with a direct ophthalmoscope

OCULOMOTOR, TROCHLEAR AND ABDUCENS – III, IV, VI

- These three nerves are tested together due to their similar functions.
- Inspect the eyelid position for ptosis (drooping). Look at the position of the upper lid relative to the iris on both sides.
- Test eye movements (*see Eye Examination page 76*)
- If you are testing the third nerve in isolation, test the pupillary responses as described earlier (since this nerve is involved in these responses also).
- Test for strabismus (squint) by performing the cover test (*see Eye Examination page 76*).
- Test for nystagmus. Ask the patient to fix their vision on your finger tip. Hold their head steady so that movement of the eye occurs. Move your finger 30° in each of the eight directions shown in the diagram, and hold it steady in each position. Watch closely for deviation of the eyes. If nystagmus is present, note the direction of the fast phase and the position of gaze in which it is maximal.

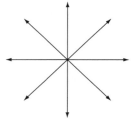

Directions in which to test for nystagmus

NB. If the eyes deviate slowly to the right and then quickly to the left, the direction of nystagmus is 'to the left'.

TRIGEMINAL – V

- Test the corneal reflex. Ask the patient to look directly in front. Using a wisp of cotton wool, approach the eye from the side and touch the cornea gently. The eyelids should blink. Test this on both sides.

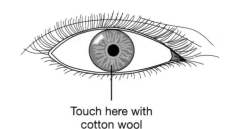

Touch here with cotton wool

Testing the corneal reflex

- Test facial sensation. Ask the patient to close their eyes and to acknowledge when they sense you touching the face. Test soft touch (with cotton wool) and pin prick sensation. Test the three divisions of the nerve on both sides by testing sensation above the eyebrows, below the eyes and on the mandible, as shown in the diagram.
- Test the jaw jerk reflex. Ask the patient to open their mouth. Rest your index finger just below the lower lip, and strike your finger gently with the patella hammer. A positive jaw jerk is present if the mandible 'jerks' upwards.
- Ask the patient to clench and unclench their teeth while palpating the masseter and temporalis muscles.

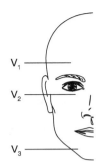

The 3 divisions of the trigeminal nerve

- Test the power of jaw opening and closing by asking the patient to resist your movements as you attempt to close the opened jaw, and open the closed jaw.
- Test the power of jaw deviation. Ask the patient to open their mouth, deviate the jaw to one side and try to hold it in that position. The examiner should try to push the jaw back into the central position. Repeat with the jaw deviated towards the other side.

FACIAL – VII

- It is usually acceptable to assess taste by asking the patient whether they have noticed a change in the taste of food. If taste in the anterior 2/3 of the tongue is to be formally assessed, ask the patient to stick out their tongue, and ask them to distinguish between salt and sugar. Test both sides of the tongue independently, and ask the patient to identify the taste before the tongue is retracted into the mouth.
- Test facial movements by asking the patient to frown and to show their teeth.
- Testing the ability to frown is a good way to distinguish between upper and lower motor neurone lesions affecting this nerve. In a lower motor neurone problem, this ability is lost on the side of the affected nerve.

- Test the power of facial movement by asking the patient to close their eyes tightly and to resist your attempt to open them. You should also attempt to part the patient's lips with your fingers after instructing them to try to keep their mouth closed.

VESTIBULOCOCHLEAR – VIII

- Crudely examine the patient's hearing using the whisper test. If the test picks up an abnormality, assess hearing further using Rinné's and Weber's tests (*see Ear Examination page 73*).
- If this nerve is being assessed in isolation, nystagmus should be tested for as described earlier.
- Balance should be tested if indicated

GLOSSOPHARYNGEAL AND VAGUS – IX, X

- These nerves are assessed together
- Note the patient's voice and ability to cough
- Ask the patient to swallow some water and note any nasal regurgitation
- Shine a light in the patient's mouth and ask them to say 'Ah.' Note the position of the uvula (i.e. central or deviated to one side).
- Test for a gag reflex by gently touching both sides of the oropharynx with a tongue depressor. Compare sensitivity and degree of palatal contraction between sides.

ACCESSORY – XI

- Inspect the sternomastoid muscles and feel their bulk
- Ask the patient to look over each shoulder in turn and to try to hold their head in that position while you attempt to turn the head back towards the midline.
- Test both muscles together by asking the patient to bring their chin to their chest and to resist your movement as you try to push the head up again.
- Test the trapezius muscles by asking the patient to hold their shoulders in a shrugged position, while you attempt to push them down.

HYPOGLOSSAL – XII

- Look at the tongue relaxed in the mouth for fasciculation, a sign of a lower motor neurone lesion.
- Ask the patient to stick out their tongue. Inspect the tongue and assess movement and any deviation.
- Test power by asking the patient to press out on the cheek with their tongue while you attempt to press it back towards the midline.

PERIPHERAL NERVES

There are six main parts to this examination.

Components of PNS examination

- Inspection
- Tone
- Power
- Co-ordination
- Reflexes
- Sensation

✓ *It is critical that you compare sides as you go along.*

INSPECTION

Ensure that the patient is adequately exposed and as relaxed as possible. Inspect for tremor, muscle wasting, muscle hypertrophy, asymmetry and abnormal posture. The examiner should also look for fasciculation (abnormal involuntary contraction of muscle fibres). If fasciculation is not obvious, you should gently flick the main muscle groups with your index finger and observe closely. It may take over one minute to demonstrate fasciculation, but this time should be cut short in an examination setting.

Pronator drift test

Ask the patient to hold their arms out at around 135° to the body, with the palms facing upwards and the fingers spread apart. The patient should then close their eyes. If one arm drops and pronates (palm turns to face the floor), the test is positive indicating that a pyramidal weakness is present.

TONE

Firstly ask the patient if they have any pain in the limb you are going to test. If you are examining the upper limb passively, move the limb through all shoulder movements, then progress to elbow flexion and extension. Next hold the patient's hand as if you were going to shake hands, and test pronation and supination. You should also quickly perform wrist extension and flexion as well as finger movements. Try to assess whether the tone is normal, increased or decreased.

Palms Up

Pronator Drift Test

Classification of increased tone

- Lead pipe (increased tone throughout movement)
- Cog wheel (ratchet-like movement)
- Clasp knife (increased tone which suddenly gives way)

Remember to compare both sides. If the patient reports a problem on one side, the normal side should be assessed first.

The principle is the same in the lower limb. Ask the patient to lie on a couch. Check that the examination will not cause pain and then with the leg straight, roll the leg from side to side. Next, lift up the leg just above the knee and allow it to drop back onto the bed. Normally the leg should drop easily back into position. With increased tone the lower leg may move abnormally. Check the tone at the ankle joint by extending and flexing. Finally flex and extend the toes. Again, remember to test both sides.

It is also important to test for clonus in the lower limb. If present, this sign is indicative of increased tone. Flex and extend the foot a few times gently, and then suddenly dorsiflex (point towards the head) the foot at the ankle joint.

✓ *Hold the foot in this position for several seconds.*

If clonus is present, you will feel the foot pushing back against your hand in a regular fashion for more than five 'beats'. It is important to remember that in some people, a few beats of clonus can be normal.

POWER

It is possible to test power in every muscle group, but this is not done routinely. The major muscle groups described below are always tested to assess power. When deciding how powerful a muscle group is, the Medical Research Council grading system is used.

Medical Research Council Power Grading System

Grade 0   No muscular contraction
Grade 1   Muscle contraction but no movement
Grade 2   Movement with gravity eliminated
Grade 3   Movement against gravity
Grade 4   Movement against gravity and resistance
Grade 5   Normal power

A particular difficulty when testing power is getting the patient to follow your instructions. This is best overcome by practising the technique and working out what you will say to the patient beforehand. **All testing of muscle power is essentially the patient trying to resist your force.**

When performing these tests it is best to compare sides as you go along i.e. test right shoulder abduction then left shoulder abduction, and so on. If the muscle group is weak, you may have to test the movement with gravity eliminated. This may require the patient to change body position, e.g. they should lie on their side for hip flexion and extension.

In the upper limb, begin by testing the shoulder abductors. Ask the patient to abduct the shoulders to 90° and to hold the arms in that position while you attempt to push the arms back against the body.

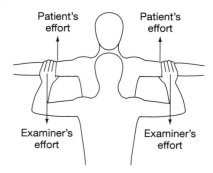

Testing power of shoulder abduction

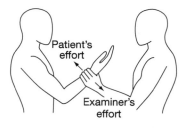

Testing power of elbow flexion

Next, test the elbow flexors. Ask the patient to flex the elbows and to keep them flexed while you attempt to straighten the arm.

Test the elbow extensors by asking the patient to keep their arm straight while you try to bend it.

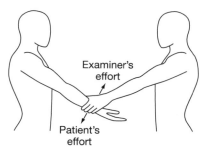

Testing power of elbow extension

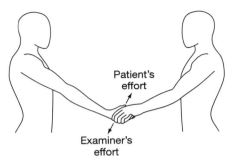

Move onto the wrist, and assess wrist flexion and extension in a similar manner to the elbow.

Testing power of wrist flexion

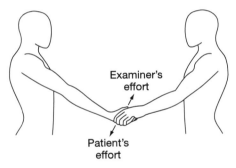

Testing power of wrist extension

Next, test power of finger abduction by asking the patient to fan out their fingers while you try to squeeze them back together.

> ✓ **When you are squeezing, press on the proximal phalanx of the index and little finger (i.e. close to the knuckle).**

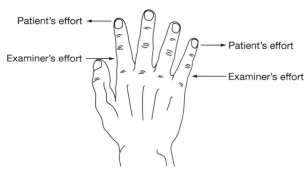

Testing power of finger abduction

Test power of finger adduction by asking the patient to hold a piece of paper between their index and middle fingers while you try to remove it.

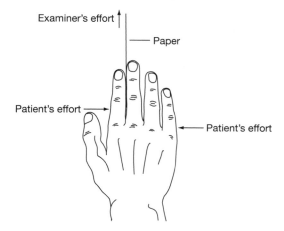

Testing power of finger adduction

In the lower limb, begin by assessing the hip flexors. Ask the patient to keep their legs straight and to raise them off the bed. You should then press down on the leg above knee level and attempt to press the leg back onto the bed.

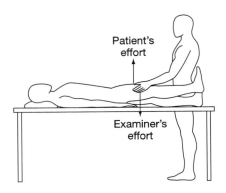

Testing power of hip flexion

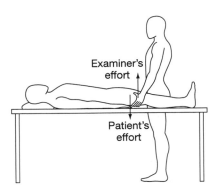

To test hip extension, first slip your hand under the patient's leg, just above the knee. Ask the patient to press your hand into the bed, while you try to lift the patient's leg off the bed.

Testing power of hip extension

Next test knee flexion and extension as shown in the diagrams. When testing knee extension, it is necessary to support the patient's leg.

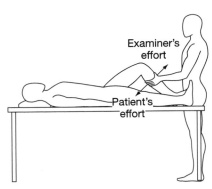

Testing power of knee flexion

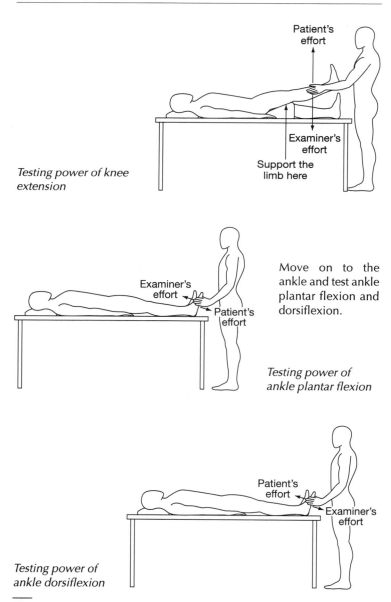

Testing power of knee extension

Move on to the ankle and test ankle plantar flexion and dorsiflexion.

Testing power of ankle plantar flexion

Testing power of ankle dorsiflexion

Next test great toe flexion and extension in a similar manner to the ankle movements. (Extension points the toe towards the head; flexion points it away.)

Finally, test toe abduction by asking the patient to fan out the toes. Toe adduction can be tested using a piece of paper in a similar manner to testing finger adduction.

> ✓ *It is a good idea to feel the muscle group that you are testing while you are assessing it. For example, if you are testing elbow flexion, rest one hand on the bulk of the biceps muscle while the other hand attempts to straighten the arm. This will catch out the patient who is not making an attempt to move!*

CO-ORDINATION

Finger-nose test

Hold your index finger one arm's length away from the patient. Ask the patient to touch your finger, then their nose, then your finger, and so on. Slowly, move your finger from side to side, and encourage the patient to move as quickly as possible. Watch the patient's hand closely for an intention tremor, dysmetria (pointing past the target) or ataxia (inco-ordination). Repeat this with their other hand.

Test for dysdiadochokinesia (difficulty performing alternating tasks)

Ask the patient to hold their left hand out with the palm upwards. They should be instructed to alternately touch the palm of this hand with the palm and then dorsum of the right hand. Encourage the patient to perform this alternating movement as quickly as possible, ensuring that the two hands are completely separated between movements. A difficulty in performing this action may indicate dysdiadochokinesia. This test should then be conducted on the other side.

Heel-shin test

Examination of co-ordination in the lower limb involves asking the patient to lie out flat on the couch. The heel of one foot should be placed on the contralateral shin, just below the knee. The patient should then run the heel down this leg towards the ankle. When this movement is complete, the patient should lift the heel off the leg and replace it on the upper shin again. This series of movements should be repeated several times, before being tested on the other side.

Gait and Romberg's test

Ask the patient to walk and note any instability or abnormal movements. Also assess the length of stride and the width of base.
Have the patient stand with the heels together, eyes open, then closed. Instability on closing the eyes (Romberg test positive) is indicative of a problem with proprioception.

REFLEXES

> ✓ **When testing reflexes, it is important that the patient is relaxed. Encourage them to let the limb 'go loose' or 'floppy' when you are testing. Utilise the full pendulum action of the hammer by holding it near the end. Allow the hammer to fall under its own weight to ensure consistency between tests. Before striking, line up the hammer on the skin over the tendon.**

In the upper limb begin with the **biceps reflex**. Ask the patient to flex their elbow to 90°, and to rest their forearm on their abdomen. Feel for the biceps tendon with one hand and rest your thumb on top of it. Strike your thumb with the patella hammer, and watch the biceps muscle for any contraction. Go on to test the other side.

Triceps reflex. Ask the patient to position their arm as before and strike the triceps tendon directly, just above the olecranon process (at the elbow). Watch for contraction of the triceps muscle. Repeat on the other side.

Supinator reflex. Keep the patient's arm in the same position. Rest your thumb or finger over the lower radius on the extensor aspect of the arm, and strike with the tendon hammer. Watch for movement in the arm.

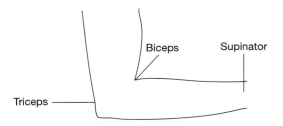

Positions for testing reflexes in the upper limb

Finger jerk **reflex**. Take all four of the patient's fingers loosely in your hand. Strike *your* fingers once with the patella hammer as shown in the diagram. If this reflex is present, you will feel the patient's fingers flexing against yours.

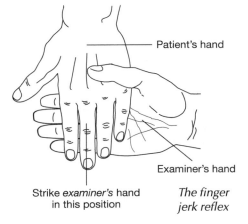

Strike *examiner's* hand in this position

The finger jerk reflex

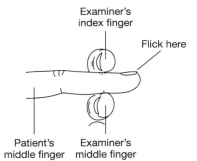

Hoffman reflex

Hoffman reflex. Support the middle phalanx of the patient's middle finger between your index and middle fingers. Flick the distal phalanx of the patient's finger with your thumb. Watch for flexion of the patient's thumb. This may indicate increased reflexes, but is also present in some normal individuals.

In the lower limb, begin by testing for a **knee jerk**. Support the patient's legs by placing your arm under their flexed knees (flexed to about 135°). Strike the patella hammer just below the knee on the patellar tendon. Watch for contraction of the quadriceps muscles.

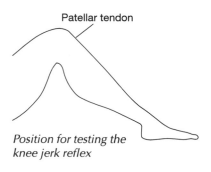

Position for testing the knee jerk reflex

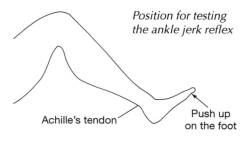

Position for testing the ankle jerk reflex

Achille's tendon

Push up on the foot

Next test the reflexes at the **ankles**. With the knees still flexed, ask the patient to let their legs fall down to the sides so that the leg lies on the bed (i.e. externally rotate the hip). Press upwards on the sole of their foot with one hand to stretch the Achilles' tendon and, with the other hand, strike the tendon with the patella hammer. Watch for contraction of the gastrocnemius muscle.

Finally assess the **plantar reflexes**. Warn the patient that the test will be uncomfortable. Use a pointed object (e.g. the spike at the end of the patella hammer or a key – make sure it's not too sharp!) and starting at the heel, run the point up the lateral border of the foot; just below the toes run the point medially (this should be done quickly). When you are doing the test, watch the patient's great toe carefully.

> ✓ *Record the very first movement of this toe as either upwards or downwards.*

Direction used to test plantar reflexes

If you are unable to elicit a tendon reflex, you should try again using a technique called 'reinforcement'. In either the upper or lower limb, ask the patient to clench their teeth hard just before you test for the reflex. In the lower limb, it is also possible to ask the patient to interlock the fingers of both hands together and then pull tight just before you test the reflex. If you are still unable to elicit the reflex after a couple of attempts with reinforcement, move on to the next stage in the examination and record that you were unable to elicit the reflex.

Spinal roots tested in reflex examination

- Biceps   C5, C6
- Triceps   C6, C7, C8
- Supinator   C6, C7
- Hoffman   C7, C8
- Knee   L2, L3, L4
- Ankle   S1, S2

SENSATION

It is important that you test sensation in all modalities.

Modalities of sensation

- Light touch
- Pain
- Two point discrimination
- Temperature
- Vibration
- Joint position sense (proprioception)

Test light touch and pain together. Use a cotton wool ball for light touch and a sharp point for pain. Show the patient the materials before you use them and touch the patient on the sternum with them so they can appreciate what they feel like.

Ask the patient to close their eyes, while you touch them with either the cotton wool or the point. The patient should identify which material is being used. Test each dermatome with both sensations in the limb being tested. Vary which material you touch the patient with to reduce the chance of them guessing correctly. If the patient is unable to distinguish between the two materials, touch them sequentially with both objects and ask if they can appreciate which one is sharper. If an abnormality is found, its distribution should be mapped out. In particular, you should record the position where the sensation returns to normal.

To test two-point discrimination, use two blunt points. Try to determine how closely you can touch the two points together on the patient's skin while they still recognise the sensation as being from two points. If the points are too close, the patient will only be aware of being touched by a single point. The distance will vary depending on where the test is carried out e.g. two points will be discriminated much closer on the finger tips than on the back.

To test temperature, special bottles can be used. One should be filled with cold water and the other with warm water. The patient should be asked to identify which is hot and which is cold. In practice, these bottles are seldom available for use. You should therefore take a cold object (such as a metal tuning fork) and ask the patient if they can sense that it is cold.

A large tuning fork is used to test vibration sensation. The fork should be struck and the non-vibrating end pressed against a bony prominence such as the medial malleolus. Ask the patient if they can feel the vibration. Then repeat the test several times, sometimes not striking the fork, and ask the patient to identify whether or not it is vibrating. If the patient is not able to identify the vibration, move more proximally on the limb.

Joint position sense is first assessed in the thumb and great toe.

✓ Grasp the patient's finger at the sides, NOT above and below.

Move the distal phalanx up and down and explain to the patient what you are doing. Now, ask the patient to close their eyes and identify whether you are moving the digit up or down. Repeat this several times to ensure that the patient is not guessing. If this sensation is intact, the examination can stop here. If it is impaired, move proximally and repeat the test in the next large joint e.g. wrist/ankle.

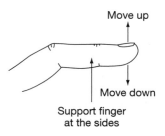

Move up

Move down

Support finger at the sides

Technique used to assess proprioception

EAR

INSPECTION

- Check for a hearing aid and, if present, ask the patient to remove it. Also note the presence of a cochlear implant or prosthesis.
- Examine the ear pinna. Note the presence of any scars. A postauricular scar may indicate mastoid surgery, whereas an endaural scar may indicate middle ear surgery. Note also any lesions on the skin of the pinna and external auditory meatus.

PALPATION

- Pull gently on the pinna and ask the patient if the movement caused pain.
- Palpate for cervical lymphadenopathy. Check the parotid, pre- and posterior- auricular nodes (*see Lymph Nodes Examination page 89*).

EXAMINATION OF EAR CANAL AND TYMPANIC MEMBRANE

- Fit a suitably sized speculum (largest feasible) to an auriscope. Before inserting this instrument into the external auditory meatus, it is necessary to straighten the ear canal by pulling on the pinna gently. In adults, the pinna should be pulled postero-superiorly, whereas in children, it should be pulled postero-inferiorly as shown below.

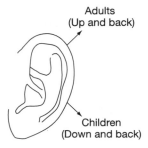

Adults
(Up and back)

Children
(Down and back)

Direction to gently pull the pinna to straighten the ear canal

- The auriscope should be held like a pen, and the little finger of the hand holding the device should be extended. When the auriscope is inserted into the ear, the little finger should rest on the patient's cheek. This way, if the patient moves their head towards you, your whole hand is also moved, thus preventing the auriscope from entering too far into the ear canal.
- Slowly insert the auriscope looking at the skin of the ear canal whilst entering.
- Inspect the tympanic membrane; look at its appearance and position.
- Examine the attic, and look in the posterosuperior canal wall for an open mastoid cavity.
- Slowly retract the auriscope from the ear

HEARING TESTS

Whisper Test

- Ask the patient to rub the external auditory canal of one ear with their finger while you test the other ear.
- Stand about 60 cm from the patient, out of their line of vision and whisper a number. Whisper at the end of your breath to try to give a repeatable test. Good numbers to use are 100 and 68 since these assess a range of frequencies.
- Ask the patient to repeat this number
- Repeat the test on the other ear

The next two tests require the appreciation that a healthy ear can hear sounds transmitted in the air better than those conducted by bone. This is because the ossicles in the middle ear amplify sound waves in the air.

Rinné's Test

- Strike a 512 Hz tuning fork; place the handle end of the fork on the patient's mastoid process. After a few seconds, move it so that the vibrating part is adjacent to the ear canal.

- Ask the patient at which point the noise is loudest.
- If the patient is unable to decide which is louder, the fork should be struck again. It is again held against the mastoid process, but this time the patient is asked to inform the doctor of the point when they can no longer hear the tone. At this moment, the tuning fork is moved in front of the ear canal, and the patient asked if they can again hear the tone.

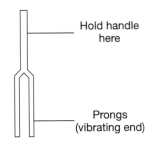

Hold handle here

Prongs (vibrating end)

Main parts of a tuning fork

If the patient has normal hearing they should hear the tone loudest when the tuning fork is placed next to the ear canal. If they are unable to tell which tone is loudest, during the second test the tone will 'reappear' when the tuning fork is moved beside the ear canal. This is known as Rinné positive (normal).

However, it should be remembered that patients with partial sensorineural (nerve) deafness will also be Rinné positive. This is because all sounds are conducted to the brain via nerves, and if these nerves are damaged, both air and bone conduction are reduced.

If the patient has conductive deafness, the amplification system in the middle ear is defective. This means that the tone is heard loudest when the tuning fork is against the mastoid process. This is known as a Rinné negative.

Problems can arise if a patient has complete unilateral sensorineural hearing loss. It may be expected that both air and bone conduction would be wiped out with this problem. However, a patient with this condition will be able to hear the tuning fork when it is placed on the mastoid process, but will not be able to hear it at all when it is placed at the ear canal. This is because with bone conduction, the sound is conducted to the other ear where it is heard. Thus, the patient in this instance will produce a Rinné negative result. However, since they do not have a conductive deafness, this is known as a 'false negative Rinné'.

In order to distinguish between a true and false Rinné, the following test can be carried out.

Weber's Test

- A similar tuning fork to that used before is again struck.
- The base of the fork is placed in the centre of the forehead. The patient is asked to inform the doctor if the sound is heard equally in the two ears, or whether it is louder in one.

In normal subjects, the sound is conducted by the bone to both ears where it is heard equally.

If a patient has a conductive deafness in one ear, the background noise normally picked up by that ear is not heard. Bone conduction is equal in both ears. This means that because the hearing defect masks out the background noise on that side, the tone is in fact heard loudest on the side of the defective ear.

If a patient has a sensorineural deafness on one side, both air and bone conducted noise are reduced. Thus, in this condition, the sound will be heard loudest on the side of the good ear.

Summary of results in Rinné's and Weber's tests

	Rinné	Weber: loudest in
Normal hearing	+ve	Both ears
Left conductive deafness	−ve	Left ear
Left partial sensorineural deafness	+ve	Right ear
Left complete sensorineural deafness	−ve	Right ear

EYES

Examination of the eye is often performed in clinical practice. Commonly, specific signs are looked for when performing an examination of a body system. For example, the sclera are examined for jaundice in the examination of the alimentary system. However, it is also necessary to be able to examine the eye in isolation.

INSPECTION

Generally

- Look for: obvious signs of systemic disease which might affect the eyes; spectacles; white stick; guide dog.

Eyes

- Look for: a glass eye; contact lenses; redness and its distribution; pupil size, shape and equality between sides; abnormal positioning of the eyes; proptosis (protrusion of the eye); strabismus (squint).

Eyelids

- Look at the positions of the lids for ptosis (drooping), retraction or other abnormalities e.g. ectropion (turning out) or entropion (turning in).

Eyebrow

- Examine for abnormalities (e.g. thinning of the outer third may be seen in hypothyroidism).

TEST VISUAL ACUITY

Snellen's chart (for distance vision)

- A standard Snellen's chart should be read from a distance of six metres (although in small rooms, the chart is usually three metres away from the patient with a mirror being used to effectively double this distance).
- Each eye is tested in turn by asking the patient to cover the eye not being tested.
- Assess acuity with distance glasses on, or contact lenses in, if appropriate. If the patient has forgotten their glasses, the test can be performed while looking through a pin hole.
- Start at the top of the chart (largest letters)
- Point to a row and ask the patient to identify the letters
- Record the minimum size of print that the patient can see with each eye
- Visual acuity is recorded in a standard fashion. For example, an acuity of 6/12 indicates that the patient can read letters from a distance of six metres that a patient with perfect eyesight would be able to read at 12 metres.

✓ *A small number is usually printed next to the row of letters being tested indicating the distance at which the letters would be able to be read by a patient with perfect visual acuity.*

- Smaller Snellen's charts are available which enable visual acuity to be assessed from the end of the bed.

Near vision test

- This test is carried out in much the same fashion as the Snellen's chart test.
- The patient is given variously sized pieces of text, with the aim of recording the smallest sized text that they can read.

Ishihara pseudoisochromatic plates (for colour vision)

- The patient is given pictures made up of various colours
- The patient must identify what number is contained in the patterns
- The aim of this test is to identify colour blindness, since different patterns of colour blindness may result in different numbers being seen, or not being seen.

ASSESS PUPILLARY RESPONSES

Response to light

- Rest the ulnar aspect of your hand on the patient's nose to stop light being shone into both eyes.
- Ask the patient to focus on an object in the distance
- Look at the size of the right pupil
- Shine the light from a pen torch into the right eye and watch for pupil constriction (direct response).
- Repeat this procedure for the left eye
- Next, look at the left pupil, whilst shining the light into the right pupil. This should constrict again (consensual response).
- Finally, watch the right pupil while you shine the light into the left eye.

Response to accommodation

- Ask the patient to focus on an object in the distance
- While they are still looking at this point, place your index finger close to the patient (approximately 10 cm away), midway between the eyes.

- While watching the size of the right pupil, ask the patient to shift their point of focus to your finger. The pupil should constrict.
- Repeat this again watching for constriction in the left pupil

ASSESS EYE MOVEMENTS

- Eye movements are assessed by asking the patient to follow your hand movements with their eyes.

> ✓ *Stabilise the patient's head with one of your hands (to ensure that their eyes are moving, not their head).*

- Hold up one finger directly in front of the patient, about 50 cm away from their face.
- Ask the patient to follow your finger with their eyes as you move through the main positions of gaze.
- In order that all positions are tested, the following system may be helpful.
- Move your hand through the shape of the letter 'H'. This will test horizontal movement, as well as up and down gaze to the left and right.
- Next, return to the centre, and move your hand through the shape of the letter 'X'. This will test diagonal movement of the eyes in all positions.
- Finally, return to the centre again, and trace the shape of the letter 'I' (i.e. vertically up and down). Firstly ask the patient look upward; then, move to a downward gaze slowly. As well as watching the eye movements here, look at the movement of the upper eyelid. It should drop down at approximately the same speed as the eye (lid lag is present if the lid movement lags behind the eye movement – this is seen with some thyroid disorders).
- Ask the patient if they experienced double vision (diplopia) in any of the directions of gaze.

ASSESS VISUAL FIELDS

- Visual fields may be tested using confrontation. On paper, the technique for confrontation seems a little laborious. However, in practice, once this is mastered, it can be performed very efficiently.

- The seating arrangements of examiner and patient are crucial if visual fields are to be assessed adequately (see diagram below).

✓ **Sit on a chair directly opposite the seated patient, so that your eyes are level with the patient's and you are about 1 metre apart.**

- The aim is to make movements with your hands which the patient is asked to identify, in order to assess whether the patient's visual fields are comparable to your's (assumed to be normal). Thus, it is vital that your hands are held midway between yourself and the patient.

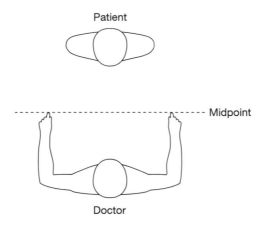

Seating arrangements for confrontation (viewed from above)

- Place your arms as shown in the diagram. Reach your left arm upwards so that your left hand is seen in the upper temporal (lateral) quadrant of your left eye. Reach your right arm downwards so that it is seen in the lower temporal quadrant of your right eye.
- Ask the patient to look directly at your nose and to close one eye. You (the examiner) should look at the patient's nose and close the opposite eye to the patient (i.e. if the patient closes their right eye, you should close your left eye). Encourage the patient to concentrate on looking at your nose for the duration of the examination and not to be tempted to look at your hands.

- Inform the patient that you are going to be moving the fingers of either your left or right hand. Ask the patient to identify (by pointing or otherwise) on which hand the fingers are being moved.
- The aim is to move your hands inwards from the periphery so that you can just see the fingers of the hand moving. When your hand is at this point, it is at the edge of your visual field.
- To do this, bring your left hand very slowly downward and towards the nose (always keeping the hand at an equal distance between you and the patient). Wiggle your index finger and stop moving your hand when you can just see your finger moving. If the patient's visual fields are identical to yours, they should also be able to see your fingers at this point. If they cannot, continue to move your hand downward and towards the nose until they notice the movement. Assess whether or not the limit of the patient's visual field is significantly different from your's.
- Next, move your right hand in a similar manner. This time move upward and towards the nose. Note the point at which you can see your finger moving, and compare this to that reported by the patient.
- Repeat these movements several times, alternating on which of the hands the finger is moved. Ensure that the patient can correctly identify on which hand the finger is being moved, and try to accurately determine the limits of these visual quadrants. Occasionally, move the fingers on both hands (to test for visual inattention).
- Next, reach your left arm downward so that your left hand is seen in the lower quadrant of the eye, and reach your right arm upward so that the right hand is seen in the upper quadrant of the eye. Assess visual fields in these quadrants in a similar fashion.
- Once all four quadrants have been tested, a central scotoma (blind area) can be examined for. A hat pin with a red head is commonly used for this purpose. This should be held laterally and slowly moved in the midline (i.e. between upper and lower fields) towards the nose. The patient should be asked to identify any regions in which they are unable to see the red part of the pin. *NB. a small 'blind spot' is present in all individuals, but this area can be much larger with certain eye problems.*
- Once these tests are complete, both patient and examiner should switch eyes and assess the visual fields in the second eye.

FUNDOSCOPY

- Warn the patient that you will get very close to their face during the examination, and also that the light from the direct ophthalmoscope is quite bright. They should be instructed to warn you if the examination becomes uncomfortable. The patient should remove their spectacles.
- Fundoscopy is much easier if the pupil has been dilated with a mydriatic drug.
- To examine the patient's right eye, hold the direct ophthalmoscope in your right hand, and look through it with your right eye. Similarly, use your left side to examine the patient's left eye.
- Ask the patient to look straight ahead.
- If possible, switch the ophthalmoscope light beam to a large circle, to enable optimal viewing.
- Stand about one metre away from the patient and look through the ophthalmoscope at the eye. If the pupil appears red, the 'red reflex' is present.
- Focus the instrument to give a clear image
- While still looking through the device, move closer to the patient, until the ophthalmoscope is close to the eye (2–3 cm away).

✓ *Reach out with the hand not holding the ophthalmoscope, and gently support the patient's upper eyelid in the open position (to prevent blinking from obstructing your examination).*

- Once you are close to the patient, use the focus control on the ophthalmoscope to obtain a sharp image of the fundus. Correct for any refractive error in your own, or the patient's eyesight.
- Identify a blood vessel, and follow its course (as it gets bigger) until you can see the optic disc.
- Note the following features of the optic disc: size, colour, cup/disc ratio, margins (distinct or blurred).
- Follow each of the major blood vessels along its course, starting at the optic disc. Note the features listed in the table opposite.
- Scan the retina in all four quadrants. Note any abnormalities of the retina.

- Ask the patient to look directly at the light, in order that you can assess the macula.
- Repeat the above process on the other eye.

Features of retinal blood vessels (4 C's)

- Calibre (normal, narrowed)
- Colour (normal, orange, white)
- Course (undulating, tortuous)
- Crossing of arterioles and veins (note the angle of crossing and whether or not the vein appears to be nipped by the artery)

SLIT LAMP EXAMINATION

The slit lamp is used primarily for examining the anterior segment of the eye. You should familiarise yourself with the workings of the lamp in order to be able to use it efficiently. However, the slit lamp will not always be available for use.

- Ask the patient to position themselves correctly for the examination. Their chin should be placed on the rest, and the forehead supported.
- Adjust the light beam so that a ray of light is evident on the patient's eye.
- Look through the eyepieces.
- Adjust the lamp until you can see a focused image.
- Select an appropriate beam of light for what you are examining e.g. use a wide beam for scanning large areas, and a narrow beam for examining smaller details.
- Angle the beam of light obliquely across the cornea. This should permit estimation of the corneal thickness.
- Closely inspect aspects of the eye nearest the outside, e.g. eyelids, eyelashes etc., and work your way inwards towards the anterior vitreous.
- The pupillary reaction to light can also be tested. Also, look for the red reflex.

COVER/UNCOVER TEST (to detect a manifest squint)

- Ask the patient to focus on an object held about 30 cm from the eyes.
- Watch the right eye carefully, and cover up the left eye (e.g. with a piece of card).
- If the right eye moves, the patient has a 'manifest squint'. The type of squint depends on the direction in which the eye moved.
  Lateral movement (i.e. the eye turns outwards) = convergent squint
  Medial movement (i.e. the eye turns inwards) = divergent squint
  Upward movement = hypotropia
  Downward movement = hypertropia
- Remove the cover from the left eye, watch the left eye carefully, and note any movement in it as you cover the right eye.
- Repeat the test with the patient focusing at an object six metres away.
- If no squint is observed, the alternate cover test should be performed.

ALTERNATE COVER TEST (to detect a latent squint)

- Quickly alternatively cover the left and right eyes several times in succession
- Cover the right eye for a few seconds
- Remove the cover and watch the right eye closely as the cover is removed.
- If the right eye moves, the patient has a 'latent squint.' The type of squint depends on the direction in which the eye moved.
  Lateral movement   = esophoria
  Medial movement   = exophoria
  Upward movement   = hypophoria
  Downward movement = hyperphoria
- This procedure can then be repeated, covering and watching the left eye.

BREAST

It is of paramount importance when examining the breast of any patient that you show dignity and respect for what is one of the most private parts of the body. If it helps, think how you would like your mother/sister/partner to be treated if they were undergoing a breast examination. You will need to carry out this examination often, since breast cancer is the leading cause of cancer death in western women. In fact it should be part of a basic examination in female patients.

> ✔ *The breast examination should NEVER be carried out alone. A male examiner should be accompanied by a female chaperone for the benefit of himself and the patient.*

Remember that breasts naturally come in different shapes, sizes and consistencies. Also remember that they may change at different stages in the menstrual cycle. It is worth bearing in mind that a breast may be reconstructed or contain an implant.

There are five components to the examination:

Components of breast examination

- Breast
- Axillae and supraclavicular fossae
- Liver
- Lungs
- Spine

The latter four components are all locations to where breast cancer commonly spreads.

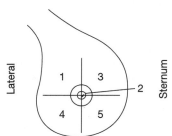

The regions of the breast showing the frequency of occurrence of neoplasia (1=most common; 5=least common)

BREAST

- Ask if there is any pain in the breasts (many ladies have sore breasts during the pre-menstrual period).
- Examine both breasts on all occasions, starting with the normal breast if an abnormality is known to be present.

Inspection

- Expose the breasts **fully** to avoid missing any sinister signs
- The breast should be observed with the patient in **three different positions.** All assist in helping to identify any of the surface features of breast pathology.

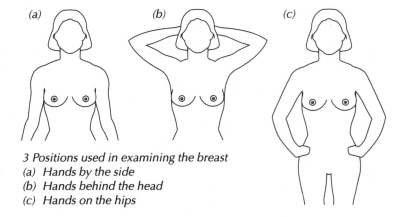

3 Positions used in examining the breast
(a) Hands by the side
(b) Hands behind the head
(c) Hands on the hips

- These positions cause tension on the underlying muscles, so features are noted that would not be evident in the normal examination position.
- Observe for: pitting, peau d'orange (resembles the dimpled skin of an orange), Paget's skin changes (looks like eczema around the nipple), puckering, in-drawing of the nipple, tethering, prominent veins.
- Look under large, pendulous breasts as you may miss scars or candidiasis in the sub-mammary folds.
- There are five features which should be noted around the nipple. These are listed in the following table.

Five D's of the nipple

- Discharge
- Discolouration
- Dermatological change
- Depression
- Deviation

Palpation

- Palpation should be done with smooth, circular, flowing movements of the fingertips. This allows the breast to be rolled between the fingers and the underlying chest wall. Be firm, but gentle, to identify any lumps.
- Squeeze the nipple gently to assess for discharge
- Use the path shown in the diagram to guide your examination
- For a lump to be palpable it must have reached 1 cm in size, by which time 1×10^9 cells will be present. If a lump is noted try and characterise it using the scheme in the following box .

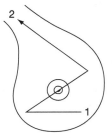

Path taken during examination of the breast (1=start point; 2=end point)

Characterisation of a breast lump (3 Ss, 3 Cs, 3 Ts)

- Site
- Size
- Shape
- Colour
- Contour
- Consistency
- Tethering
- Transillumination
- Temperature

✓ *Make sure that you palpate the axillary tail, nipple and retro-areolar areas.*

- Record any findings and add an accompanying sketch. Templates are frequently available for this purpose.

AXILLAE AND SUPRACLAVICULAR NODES

- Inspect the axillae: lumps may be apparent without palpation
- All five walls of the axillae should be examined: lateral, medial, anterior, posterior and apex (roof). You must take the weight of the patient's arm to relax the axilla.
- The examination is performed from behind the patient with movements of the fingers similar to that described above for the breast; you are trying to identify metastatic deposits.

LIVER *(see Alimentary System Examination page 13)*

- Palpation of the liver is necessary to detect metastatic disease. If extensive, the liver may be hard, craggy and irregular.

CHEST *(see Respiratory System Examination page 7)*

- The chest should be examined for the presence of a malignant pleural effusion. This is likely to be unilateral if present.
- Chest expansion, percussion, auscultation and vocal resonance should be performed.

SPINE

- You should examine the spine for tenderness that may result from metastases.

✓ Finally, you may advise the patient to examine her own breasts on a regular basis and encourage 50–64-year-olds to comply with the NHS national breast screening programme.

LYMPH NODES

It is possible that you may be asked to examine the cervical lymph nodes on their own, but, more commonly you will use this examination as part of a more thorough systems evaluation, such as the respiratory system, or in examining the head and neck or thyroid. As with other examinations, it is important to have a system. A good method to use here takes the form of a 'road map'. If you follow this map with your examining fingers, then you can be sure that all groups of lymph nodes have been assessed.

This examination is best carried out by standing behind the seated patient. Some doctors advise that both sides should be examined simultaneously; others prefer to examine each side in isolation. There are two chains of cervical lymph nodes: circular and vertical. The examination begins with the circular chain.

Diagram A represents the underside of the patient's chin and mandible. Begin at the point marked '1' (submental nodes), feeling for any abnormalities with the flats of your fingers, moving in a circular motion. Work your way round to point '2' which is at the angle of the mandible. The submandibular nodes lie at this point.

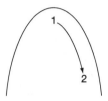

(A) Location of lymph nodes under the chin and mandible

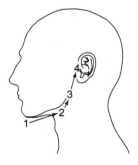

Without lifting your fingers off the patient's face, work your way to point '3' as shown in diagram B. This is the location of the parotid nodes. Continue towards point '4'. This point is directly anterior to the tragus of the ear and is the position of the preauricular node.

(B) Location of lymph nodes anterior to the ear pinna

Next, move your fingers to the posterior side of the ear pinna, and feel for the posterior auricular nodes ('5' in diagram C). When you have examined to the inferior aspect of the mastoid process, move on to the posterior aspect of the head and palpate for the occipital nodes ('6').

This completes the examination of the **circular chain** of lymph nodes.

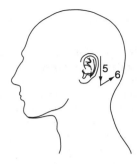

(C) Location of lymph nodes posterior to the ear pinna

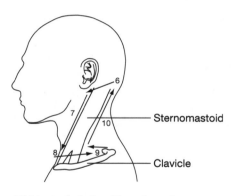

(D) Vertical chain of lymph nodes

Next, the **vertical chain** of lymph nodes must be examined (diagram D). Ask the patient to relax their shoulders. Work your way along the anterior border of the sternomastoid muscle ('7'). At its inferior end, palpate the muscle between finger and thumb to feel for the scalene node ('8').

Next, move laterally and examine the supraclavicular fossa ('9').

Finally, work your way up towards the occipital region again, by palpating the posterior border of the sternomastoid muscle and the posterior triangle of the neck ('10').

If lymphadenopathy is detected, it may be appropriate to examine other lymph node areas. These include the axillary, epitrochlear (at the elbow), inguinal and popliteal nodes. The liver and spleen should also be palpated for enlargement.

Distinguishing between the cause of a neck lump involves consideration of the anatomical location of the abnormality. The position of the lesion often narrows the differential diagnosis.

SKIN LESIONS

Often patients suffer from the 'leper complex' and are very conscious of their skin lesion. Therefore, it is important not to be reticent when examining skin lesions.

- The area to be examined should be adequately exposed. The patient should wear a hospital gown if necessary.

✓ *Ensure that the skin to be examined is well illuminated (use a lamp if necessary).*

- If appropriate, ask the patient to wash off any make-up or to remove a wig.
- Examination of a skin lesion should begin by looking at the body part offered by the patient.

There are several features to be noted.

Features of skin lesions

- Colour
- Configuration of lesions
- Distribution: e.g. flexor, extensor surfaces
- Edge: well defined, ill defined
- Geometric shape: e.g. oval, circular, irregular
- Primary lesion
- Secondary lesion
- Surface contour (*see diagram overleaf*)
- Smell: no odour, foul-smelling
- Temperature: normal, hot
- Texture: rough, smooth, hard, soft

✓ *A simple diagram or photograph of the lesion is often useful for recording its details and any change over time or in response to treatment.*

Configuration of lesions

Lesions are often found in certain configurations, as shown in the diagram.

Alternatively, the lesions may be scattered all over the body, in no particular configuration.

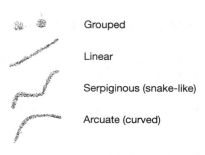

Grouped

Linear

Serpiginous (snake-like)

Arcuate (curved)

Common configurations of lesions

Primary lesion

- The lesion should be described in dermatological terms. The following words are commonly used: macule, papule, nodule, plaque, vesicle, bulla, pustule, weal, purpura, ecchymosis, telangiectasia, cyst, comedo, burrow.

Secondary lesion

- If present, the following should be described: crusting, scaling, excoriation, fissure, atrophy, striae, ulceration, lichenification, scarring.

Surface contour

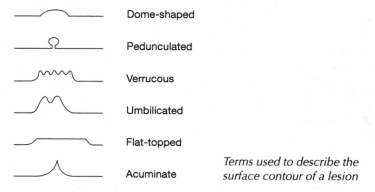

Dome-shaped

Pedunculated

Verrucous

Umbilicated

Flat-topped

Acuminate

Terms used to describe the surface contour of a lesion

General skin examination

- Ask about any other skin lesions present and examine where necessary.

> ✓ *If there are lesions on the hands, always examine the feet too,*
> *and vice versa.*
> *If there are lesions on the feet, also always examine the groin.*

It may be appropriate to look in the mouth for other signs of cutaneous disease e.g. Wickham's striae of lichen planus or white plaques of systemic candidiasis.

Examination of a skin ulcer

Examination of an area of skin ulceration deserves specific mention.

Description of a skin ulcer

- Site, size (measure and record in millimetres), shape, edge (sharp, rolled), wall (in-sloping, punched-out), floor (e.g. granulation tissue), base (mobile, sitting on bone)
- Details about the surrounding skin – both local and distant
- Examination of the regional lymph nodes should be performed
- An assessment of the peripheral pulses near the lesion should also be performed (*see Cardiovascular Examination page 1*).

THYROID

When conducting a thyroid examination, it is important to distinguish whether you want to examine the ***thyroid gland*** itself, or the ***thyroid status*** of the patient. Since thyroid dysfunction can be manifest in many body systems, it is necessary to examine more than just the gland when assessing the thyroid status of a patient.

General inspection

- Look for: weight abnormalities; irritability; signs of heat/cold intolerance (e.g. wearing shorts in winter); peaches and cream complexion; hair/eyebrow changes; voice and tongue changes; skin changes.

Inspect the hands

- Fingers: onycholysis (nail lifting off the nail bed), thyroid acropachy.
- Palms: palmar erythema, warm/cold, vasodilatation, sweatiness, signs of carpal tunnel syndrome.

Resting tremor

- Place a sheet of paper on top of the patient's outstretched hands.

Examine the radial pulse

- May possibly detect: bradycardia or tachycardia; irregularly irregular rhythm (due to atrial fibrillation).

Measure blood pressure

- May possibly detect: hypertension (especially systolic)

Test for proximal myopathy in the arms

- Press down on the patient's arms which should be positioned in the same way as when testing the power of shoulder abductors (*see Peripheral Nervous System Examination page 59*).

Examine the eyes

- Inspect (from the sides and behind): for exophthalmos (protrusion of the eye) and periorbital oedema.
- Test eye movements: watch for lid lag or lid retraction; ask the patient if they experience diplopia (*see Eye Examination page 76*).

Examine the neck

- Ask the patient if their neck is sore
- Inspect: at rest, from the front and side, with the tongue in the mouth, protruded, and during swallowing. (A thyroglossal cyst will move superiorly upon tongue protrusion.)
- Palpate the thyroid gland: stand behind the patient and palpate the whole gland. With one hand, stabilise one lobe, while the other hand palpates the other lobe. Repeat with the other hand. Finally, palpate both lobes simultaneously and palpate whilst the patient swallows.
- Check for cervical lymphadenopathy (*see Lymph Nodes Examination page 89*).

- Percuss: start at the thyroid gland and work inferiorly. A large thyroid may extend retrosternally (this will be detected as dullness to percussion).
- Auscultate each lobe for bruits while the patient holds their breath.

Test for proximal myopathy in the legs

- Ask the patient to rise from a squatting position without using their hands.

Test the knee jerk reflexes *(see Peripheral Nervous System Examination page 70)*

- May be brisk or slow relaxing ('hung up')

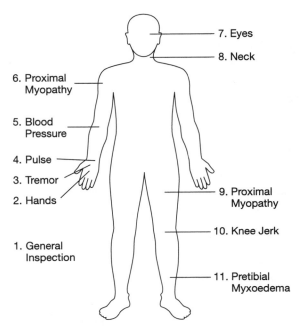

Thyroid status examination

Test for pretibial myxoedema

- Press for up to one minute on the anterior aspect of the shin, and look for dimpling.

Three signs unique to Grave's disease

- Ophthalmoplegia
- Pretibial myxoedema
- Thyroid acropachy (clubbing)

TESTES

It is important when carrying out this examination, to be mindful of the sensitivity of this area, and to appreciate that men may feel embarrassed and afraid of getting hurt. It is therefore important that the examination should be carried out very gently and with concern for the patient's dignity.

INSPECTION

- The patient should be examined in the supine position, with the scrotum drawn forward to lie on top of the thighs.
- The scrotum should be inspected on all sides, and pubic hair distribution noted. Ask if the scrotum is painful.
- Each side of the scrotum should be examined independently.

PALPATION

- The spermatic cord should be palpated between finger and thumb, and its course followed from internal inguinal ring to testis.
- The testis should be palpated next. It is important to watch the patient's face during this part of the examination to ensure that you are not causing him any pain. The testis and epididymis should be fully palpated.

- If measuring beads are available, the testicular size should be measured.
- Examination of the contralateral testis should be carried out next

To complete the examination, the inguinal regions should be palpated for lymphadenopathy.

The first key decision to be made upon finding a swelling, is whether the swelling is on the scrotum or in the scrotum. If a mass is palpated in the scrotum, the key question to ask yourself is 'can I get above it?' If it is not possible to feel the upper border of the mass, it is likely to be an inguinal hernia.

If you are able to palpate the upper border of the mass, you must then decide whether the mass is cystic or solid, and if it is separate from the testis or whether it lies within the testis. It is also possible that the testis may not be palpable because of the mass.

The final step should be to transilluminate the mass. This involves shining a bright light at the back of the mass and noting whether or not the light is transmitted. The torch should be shone through a tube held up against the mass, as shown in the diagram.

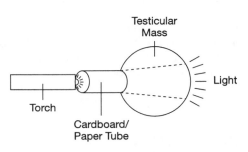

Transillumination of a testicular mass

Noting the patient's age and taking a history are also important parts of deciding the cause of testicular pathology.

VAGINA

Due to the intimate nature of this examination it is imperative that it is carried out in as dignified a manner as possible. The nature of the examination should be well explained before the patient is examined, and consent obtained. It is recommended that the vagina is referred to as 'the front passage', since some women may not be familiar with the term 'vagina'.

✓ *A female chaperone should always be present for this examination.*

✓ *Gloves should be worn.*

- Ask the patient to change into a hospital gown
- The patient should lie on a couch on their back
- Ask the patient to bring their feet up to their bottom, and to let their knees fall to the sides.
- Ensure that the area to be examined is adequately illuminated. A lamp should be used if necessary.

INSPECTION

- Expose the area and inspect the pubic hair, labia, clitoris and urethra. Pay particular attention to any swellings, discharge or bleeding. The peri-anal area should also be inspected for any abnormalities.

PALPATION

- Ask if there is any pain before beginning palpation, and watch the patient's face throughout the examination.
- Part the labia majora using the index and middle fingers of the left hand in a 'scissor-like' motion.
- Ask the patient to cough, and look for any discharge or abnormalities of the vaginal walls (e.g. cystocele, rectocele, prolapsed uterus).

- Gently palpate Bartholin's glands (situated at the 5 and 7 o'clock positions of the labia). Normally, these cannot be palpated. Note any tenderness or swelling.
- If appropriate, gently 'milk' the urethra, and note the presence of any discharge.

EXAMINATION WITH A BIVALVE SPECULUM

- Tell the patient that you are going to pass a small device into the front passage in order to look at the womb.
- Lubricate the speculum with some lubricating jelly.
- Inform the patient that you are about to insert the speculum. Ensure that the speculum is warmed first.
- Pass the speculum slowly, with gentle pressure exerted backwards and downwards.
- Rotate the speculum as you insert in order to follow the contour of the vagina. The device should be inserted in a vertical plane, and rotated to lie in a horizontal plane.
- When in position, open the speculum out, and inspect the cervix.
- Look at the shape and size of the cervix, and note any abnormalities, such as erosions, polyps or discharge.
- Tell the patient that you are going to remove the speculum, before doing so slowly and gently.
- You may want to take a cervical smear at this stage, if appropriate.

BIMANUAL EXAMINATION

- Inform the patient that you are going to insert two fingers into the front passage in order to feel the womb.
- Lubricate the index and middle fingers of the gloved right hand.
- Pass in the fingers gently. Rotate the fingers as you insert in order to follow the contour of the vagina. The fingers should be inserted in a vertical plane, and rotated to lie in a horizontal plane.
- Feel the cervix with the tips of your fingers (it should feel like the tip of a nose). Note any cervical excitation (pain on touching the cervix).
- Using the left hand, palpate the abdomen, starting near the xiphisternum, and moving downward.

- Try to feel the uterus between your two hands. Assess its size, shape, consistency, motility and tenderness.
- It may also be possible to palpate fallopian tubes and ovaries (Adnexa); any tenderness or other abnormalities should be noted.
- Tell the patient that you are going to remove your fingers, before doing so slowly and gently.
- Clean any lubricating jelly from the patient with a tissue.
- Thank the patient, and cover the area examined with a gown.

RECTUM

The personal nature of this examination means that it requires a detailed explanation of what will be done before beginning. Explain that the procedure may be uncomfortable, but it should not be painful. Explain that you are going to examine their 'back passage', and that this is a short procedure that should last at most 1–2 minutes. As an undergraduate, this examination is likely to be first performed on a model, although this should be treated exactly as for a real patient, with respect to examination and communication.

> ✓ *A chaperone should always be present for this examination.*

- Gloves should be worn
- Ask the patient to change into a hospital gown
- The patient should lie on a couch on their left side (left lateral position)

> ✓ **Ask the patient to bend their knees, and to bring their knees up as close to their chest as possible. They should try to position themselves so that the buttocks are as close to the edge of the couch as possible.**

- Expose the peri-anal area by lifting up the right buttock

INSPECTION

- Examine the peri-anal area for any abnormalities such as fissures, haemorrhoids, skin tags or warts.
- Ask the patient to 'strain down', and note any rectal prolapse.

PALPATION

- Lubricate the index finger of the gloved right hand using lubricating jelly.

> ✓ *Touch the peri-anal area gently, and ask the patient if any pain is felt. Inform the patient that you are going to insert your finger.*

- Gently insert your index finger into the back passage, so that the palmar aspect of the finger is oriented towards the patient's back. Note any spasm of the sphincter muscle as you insert your finger.
- Palpate the rectal wall with your finger. Watch the patient's face for any signs of pain during the examination.
- Gently and slowly, rotate your hand anticlockwise and palpate the rectal wall until the palmar aspect of your finger is facing the patient's front.
- Rotate your hand in a clockwise direction until the finger is back in the starting position. Continue to rotate the hand in a clockwise direction until the palmar aspect of the finger is again facing the patient's front.
- At the end of the examination, all areas of the rectal wall should have been palpated.
- Particular attention should be paid to the prostate gland in male patients. This is palpated through the anterior wall of the rectum.

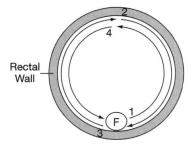

'Path' taken during palpation of the rectal wall. (F = finger starting point)

Distinguishing a benign from a malignant prostatic tumour

- Benign: smooth surface; sulcus felt
- Malignant: irregular craggy border; loss of medial sulcus

- Withdraw the finger slightly, and ask the patient to strain down again. Palpate the lower rectum for any abnormalities.
- The finger should then be totally removed
- The glove should be inspected on withdrawal for any blood, slime, stools, or other abnormality.
- To finish, clean any lubricating fluid away from the peri-anal area with a tissue.
- Thank the patient and cover the area examined with the gown.

LEVEL OF CONSCIOUSNESS

Consciousness is a state of awareness of one's self and the surrounding environment. In most medical consultations this is taken for granted as the patient is fully conscious through their engagement in history taking and examination. However, the level of consciousness can alter, especially in the emergency setting and is often indicative of a serious pathological process.

The level of detail with which one assesses and records the level of consciousness depends on the medical setting. The simplest and most applicable to a general ward is shown below.

Assessment of level of consciousness

5: Fully conscious and alert
4: Confused, but responding appropriately
3: Obeying vocal commands
2: Semi-purposeful movement to pain
1: Reflex movement to pain (withdrawal)
0: Unresponsive to pain

A good deal of terminology may be heard referring to altered states of consciousness. Levels 3 and 4 in the above scale may be referred to as, 'clouding of consciousness'. Level 2 may be considered as 'stupor' and levels 1 and 0 as being in a state of 'coma'.

> ✓ *In order to elicit pain for the purposes of this assessment there are two recognized methods. Either apply pressure over the sternum using the knuckles of a clenched hand or, using the fingers, apply pressure over the supra-orbital ridge (the top of the eye socket).*

An extremely basic and rapid system, **AVPU** may be used in emergency medicine.

AVPU use in emergency medicine

Alert   Responds to Voice   Responds to Pain   Unconscious

It may be necessary to perform a more detailed and formal assessment of a patient's conscious state, especially in emergency or intensive care departments, using the Glasgow Coma Scale. This comprises a scoring system, giving scores in three key areas: eye-opening, best motor response and best verbal response. The minimum score is 3, and the maximum is 15.

Eye Opening

1: Nil
2: Open in response to pain
3. Open in response to loud verbal commands
4: Spontaneous

Best Motor Response

1: Nil
2: Abnormal extension in response to pain
3: Abnormal flexion in response to pain
4: Withdraws body part in response to pain
5: Localizing
6: Obeys commands

Best verbal response

1: Nil   4: Confused
2: Incomprehensible   5: Orientated
3: Inappropriate

MENTAL STATE

The mental state examination is the psychiatric equivalent of a physical examination. When the presenting complaint is primarily one relating to mental health, a detailed formal assessment is undertaken. For the purposes of the general health assessment it is sufficient to use the Mini Mental State Format as detailed below. This, like the Glasgow Coma Scale (*see Level of Consciousness page 101*), follows a standardized system, giving a score out of 30, which is transferable and reproducible in any health institution. Each '*' symbol below indicates what constitutes 1 point scored for a correct answer.

Orientation

- Can you tell me today's date*, month* and year*?
- Which day of the week is it today*?
- Can you also tell me which season it is*?
- What city/town are we in*?
- What county* and country* are we in?
- What building are we in* and on what floor*?

Anterograde (short term) memory

- I would like you to remember three objects (e.g. orange, tobacco, airplane)
- Ask for the words to be repeated (registration) and score 1 for each correct word***. Repeat until all three are remembered, allowing up to six attempts. Record the number of trials needed.

Attention & calculation

- Serial 7s. Starting with the number 100, subtract 7 and repeat i.e. 100, 93, 86 Stop at 65. Score 1 for each correct number*****.

- **ALTERNATIVELY**, for those who have a dislike for numbers, ask them to spell the word 'WORLD' backwards. Score 1 for each correct letter*****.

Recall

What were the three words I asked you to remember earlier (orange, tobacco, airplane)? Score 1 for each correct word remembered ***.

Language

- Name these objects (show the patient two easily recognisable objects e.g. watch, pen)**.
- Repeat the following phrase: 'no ifs, ands or buts' *
- Read this sentence and do what it says (show card with 'CLOSE YOUR EYES' written on it). Score 1 if the patient closes their eyes*.
- Write a short, simple sentence for me (e.g. 'I went to the shops yesterday')*
- Instruct the patient to 'take a piece of paper in your left hand*, fold it in half* and put it on the floor'*
- Can you copy this drawing? (both pentagons must have 5 sides and overlap)*

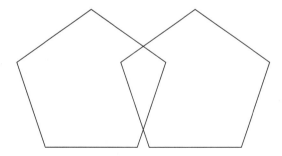

Pentagons overlapping

These 6 aspects of language test respectively: naming, repeating, reading, writing, three-stage-command and visuospatial components.

TOTAL SCORE 30

CHEST

TECHNICAL ASPECTS

- **Name and date of examination**
  Always check that it is the correct patient, and that it is the appropriately dated examination. (It's not uncommon for patients to have dozens of chest x-rays!) This is sound practice for any radiographic examination.

- **Rotation**
  The spinous processes of the vertebrae should be equidistant from the medial borders of the clavicle

- **Inspiration**
  There should be 10 posterior ribs visible in the midclavicular line on full inspiration

- **Penetration**
  The vertebral bodies should be visible through the heart shadow

REVIEW AREAS

These are structures that should be evaluated in every chest radiograph:

- Heart size and shape
- Pulmonary vasculature
- Lungs (including hila)
- Bony contours (ribs, spine, shoulders)
- Soft tissues (especially breast shadows, axillae and neck)

THE NORMAL CARDIAC OUTLINE

- **Cardiothoracic ratio**
  The maximum transverse diameter of the heart should not exceed 55% of the maximum transverse diameter of the chest

- **Right heart border**
  This shadow is formed by the (from above, downwards):
  Superior vena cava
  Right atrium
  Inferior vena cava

- **Left heart border**
  This shadow is formed by the (from above, downwards):
  Aortic knuckle
  Pulmonary trunk
  Left atrial appendage
  Left ventricle

- **Normal pulmonary vascularity**
  Discrete vessels should not be visible in the outer 1/3 of the lung fields

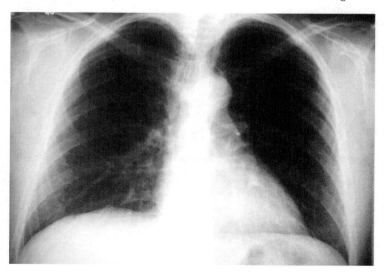

Normal CXR

CARDIAC FAILURE

- **Cardiothoracic ratio**
  The heart enlarges and the transverse diameter increases to > 0.55

- **Upward venous diversion**
  As cardiac decompensation occurs, there is upward shunting of blood so the vascularity increases. (Normally, a superior pulmonary vein, measured in the second interspace, measures < 2–3 mm.)

- **Pulmonary vascularity**
  Enlargement of the radiating vessels means that they are discretely visible in the outer 1/3 of the lung.

- **Kerley B lines**
  These are peripheral horizontal lines at the margins of the lung bases seen (but not exclusively) in cardiac failure.

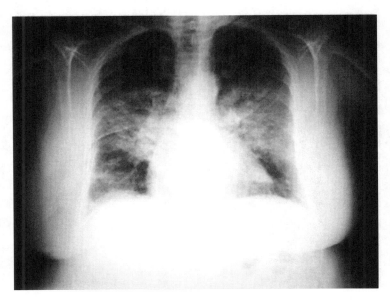

Cardiac failure

- **Air space change**
  As the pulmonary venous pressure increases beyond 25 mmHg, pulmonary oedema occurs, and the acini become consolidated. At this stage, air-bronchograms are identified, typically bilaterally and in a perihilar location.

THE DIAGNOSIS OF LOBAR PNEUMONIA

- **The silhouette sign**
  This states that the heart shadow and the diaphragm are visible because they are surrounded by air in the surrounding pulmonary acini. If lobar consolidation occurs, the adjacent acini obscure that portion of the silhouette. Opposite, the specific silhouette losses are described for the associated lobar consolidations.

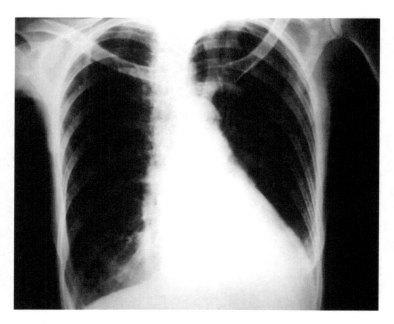

Left lower lobe pneumonia

Specific silhoutte losses with associated lobar consolidations

Right upper lobe	Right upper mediastinum
Right middle lobe	Right heart border
Right lower lobe	Right hemidiaphragm
Left upper lobe	Aortic knuckle
Lingula	Left heart border
Left lower lobe	Left hemidiaphragm

- **With ensuing lobar collapse there is:**
  Volume loss (ipsilateral)
  Diaphragmatic elevation
  Movement of the ipsilateral hilum towards the collapsed lobe

PULMONARY MASS LESION

- Localisation of perihilar lesions can be achieved by using the silhouette sign. Lesions in the middle mediastinum will obscure the adjacent heart or mediastinal shadow. Lesions in front of, or behind the heart, will allow the cardiac and mediastinal shadows to be identified despite the discrete lesion.
- Lesions above the clavicle on the frontal chest radiograph are posteriorly placed. (Always look for associated posterior rib erosion or destruction)

Lesions by location

Anterior mediastinal mass
Thymic tumours
Teratoma
Lymphoma
Retrosternal thyroid
   (look for suprasternal, contralateral tracheal displacement)

Middle mediastinal mass
Bronchogenic carcinoma
Lymphadenopathy
Aortic aneurysm

Posterior mediastinal mass
Aortic aneurysm   Neurogenic tumours
Dilated oesophagus   Paravertebral abscesses

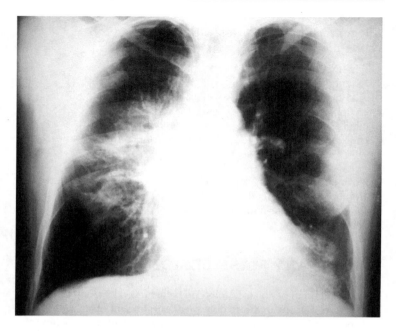

Right-sided bronchial carcinoma

PNEUMOTHORAX

- This is more easily demonstrated in the expiratory phase, when the relatively positive intrapleural pressure pushes the lung edge away from the chest wall. The lung edge is demonstrated against the relative 'blackness' of the intrapleural air.
- **Tension pneumothorax.** If there is a valve type effect, e.g. following stabbing, with each breath, more air is introduced into the pleural space, and the lung becomes progressively pushed away from the chest wall.

  Signs of tension:

  Flattening or depression of the ipsilateral hemidiaphragm

  Movement of the heart to the contralateral side

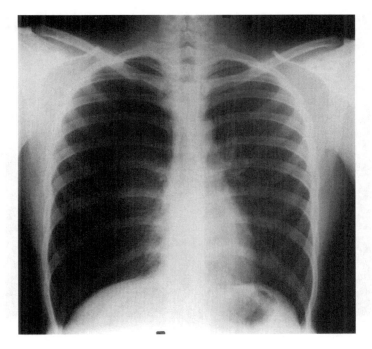

Pneumothorax

PLEURAL EFFUSION

- Loss of basal aerated lung means there is usually loss of the hemi-diaphragm's silhouette on the erect radiograph. In addition, the fluid curves upwards peripherally at the lung edge to produce a crescentic meniscus. Mass effect will displace the heart to the contralateral side (unless there is associated lobar collapse, when the mass effect of the effusion is 'neutralised' by the volume loss of the collapsed lung lobe),
- In the supine film, look for a veiled, greying of the affected side, caused by fluid lying posteriorly between the lung and the chest wall. This is a particularly crucial observation to make in an emergency trauma patient, who may have substantial volume of blood concealed in the intrapleural space.

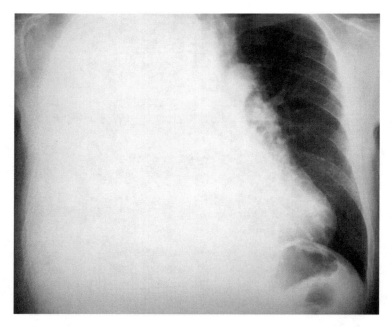

Right-sided pleural effusion completely obscuring the right lung

Key Terms

Contralateral: opposite side
Crescentic: shaped like a crescent or half moon
Equidistant: equal distance between two objects or places
Hemidiaphragm: half of the diaphragm
Intrapleural: within the pleura
Ipsilateral: same side
Lingula: superior and inferior bronchopulmonary segments, generally considered to be part of the left upper lobe
Perihilar: around the hilar region of the lung
Transverse diameter of chest: distance between the midline and the outermost limit of the thoracic cavity (measured at the widest point)

ABDOMEN

NORMAL BOWEL GAS PATTERN

- **Proportion of gas within the stomach and bowel**
  Normally gas in stomach, colon and rectum
  There is little gas in the small bowel

- **Dimensions of the jejunum and ileum**
  Wall thickness: 2–2.5 mm
  Lumen diameter: 2–3 cm

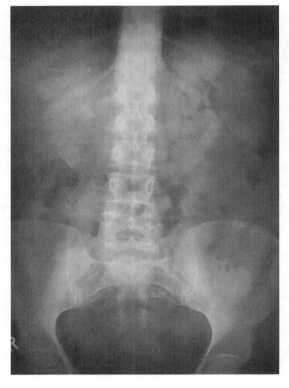

Abdominal X-ray

INTESTINAL OBSTRUCTION

- **Small bowel obstruction**
  Distended bowel centrally
  Valvulae conniventes present
  Diameter < 5cm

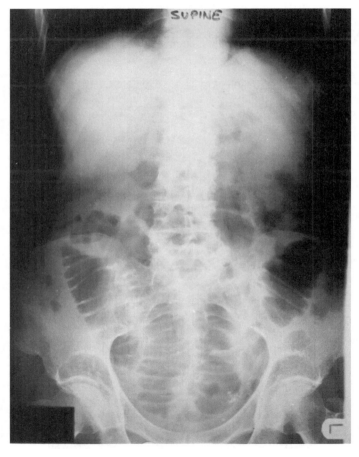

Small bowel obstruction

- **Large bowel obstruction**
  Distended bowel peripherally
  Haustra, but no valvulae
  Diameter > 5 cm

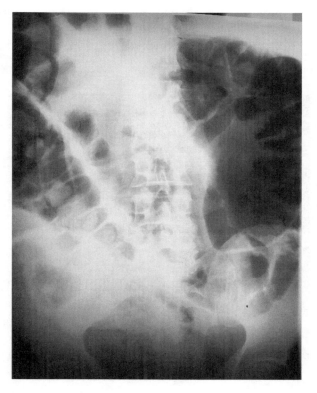

Large bowel obstruction

VOLVULUS

Any portion of bowel on a mesentery may twist about that mesentery to produce a volvulus

- **Caecal volvulus**
  Single enlarged loop
  Mostly fluid filled (high fluid/ air ratio)
  No gas in large bowel
  Younger age group (30–40 years)

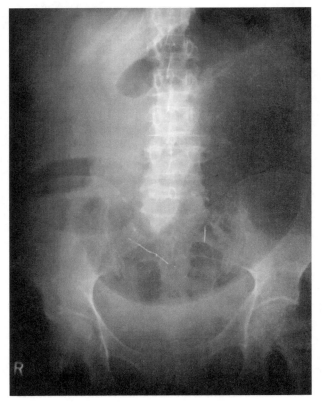

Caecal volvulus

- **Sigmoid volvulus**
  Two loops (coffee-bean sign)
  Mostly air filled (low air/fluid ratio)
  Distended large bowel
  Tapered sigmoid obstruction (bird of prey sign)
  Older age group (> 60 years)

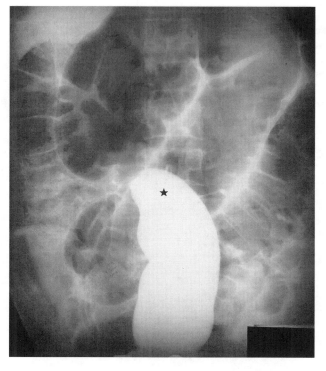

Sigmoid volvulus (single contrast enema demonstrating the bird of prey sign★)

ILEUS AND PSEUDO-OBSTRUCTION

Differentiating points from mechanical bowel obstruction

- **Intestinal obstruction**
  Abdominal pain
  Gas-filled bowel loops
  Cut-off point

- **Ileus**
  No abdominal pain
  Gas-filled bowel loops
  No cut-off point

- **Pseudo-obstruction**
  Abdominal pain
  Gas-filled bowel loops
  No cut-off point
  Differential caecal enlargement

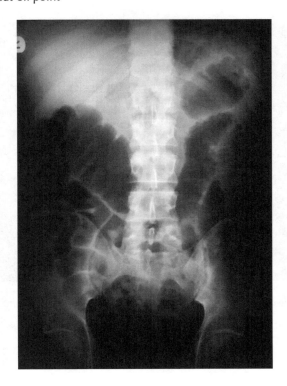

Ileus

PNEUMOPERITONEUM

- **The erect abdominal radiograph**
  Free air under diaphragm (right side more sensitive than left)

- **The supine abdominal radiograph**
  Riegler's sign (free air on both sides of the bowel wall)
  Falciform ligament sign (the sickle-shaped falciform ligament is outlined by air in a band running between the liver and the umbilicus)

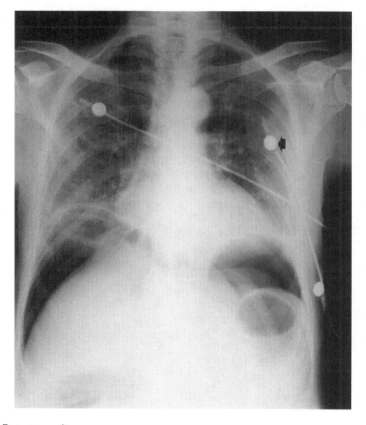

Pneumoperitoneum

INFLAMMATORY BOWEL DISEASE

- **Toxic megacolon**
  Widening of the transverse colonic lumen (>5.5cm)
  Mucosal oedema (thumbprinting)
  No residual faecal shadows (catharsis)

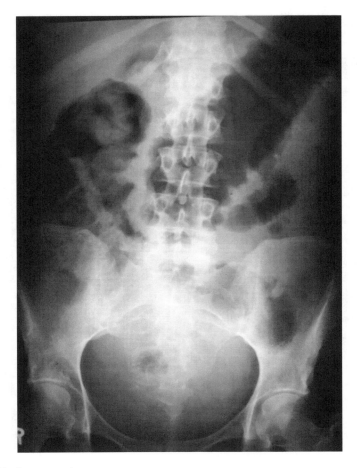

Toxic megacolon

MISCELLANEOUS

- **Hepatomegaly**
  Descent of right lobe into the right iliac fossa (RIF). Beware Riedel's lobe. (True hepatomegaly has enlargement of both lobes. Riedel's lobe typically has a normal or small left lobe.)

- **Vertebral abnormalities**
  Degeneration (spondylosis)
  Reduction of disc space
  Osteophytes at bony margins
  Sclerotic bony margins
  Malignant infiltration
  Check that both pedicles are present at each vertebral level. (Malignant infiltration destroys the pedicle first.)

- **Pathological Calcification**
  Pancreatitis
  > Flecks of calcification transversely across the upper abdomen in chronic pancreatitis (30–40%). (Calcification is rare in adenocarcinoma of the pancreas–only 2% of cases.)

- **Aortic aneurysm**
  Convex arc of calcification aligned to vertebral column. The calcification is on the endothelial surface, and therefore indicates the 'inner' diameter of the aneurysm.
  Better appreciated on the lateral x-ray.

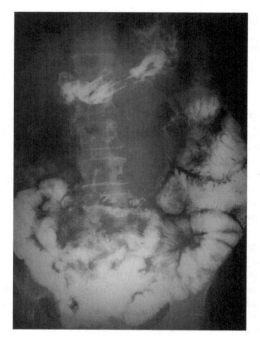

Aortic aneurysm

Key Terms

Falciform ligament: a fold of peritoneum dividing the left and right lobes of the liver, attaching it to the anterior abdominal wall and diaphragm. The free lower edge contains the ligamentum teres (obliterated left umbilical vein).

Haustra: incomplete transverse folds caused by the longitudinal colonic taenia

Riedel's Lobe: an extension of the lateral portion of the right lobe of the liver.

Valvulae conniventes: circular folds of mucous membrane in the small intestine.

Volvulus: twisting of part of the intestinal tract about its mesentery causing partial or complete obstruction.

Medical records serve several functions:

A 'Working Document'

The recorded case history is a document recorded at the time of admission and the subsequent period of days, weeks or months of the patient's stay. It is used to record actual findings, results of tests, plans for future investigation, information received from relatives, health care workers and other interested parties and also how, why and when decisions were made regarding treatment options or changes to therapy.

A Permanent Record of a Clinical Event

The recording then serves as a permanent record of an event in time that can be rediscovered and assessed. This is of use during outpatient follow-up.

A Reference Document for Other Staff

Patients admitted to hospital meet a variety of clinical staff and a team of junior doctors often undertake their medical management. The medical record is central to providing information that can be shared by all the medical staff involved. Provided records are updated and accurate, it facilitates continuity of care for the patient and allows staff to quickly become familiar with events which may have happened of which they were not aware.

A Historical Record of Past Events

Some illnesses evolve over a period of weeks, months or even years. Occasionally it is only by reviewing past medical records of isolated acute events that one can appreciate how an illness is evolving and realise the underlying diagnosis.

A Legal Document

Unfortunately this is becoming more and more important. Patients rightly expect the best clinical care from the medical profession. Sometimes patients or their relatives feel that the care and attention that was given was less than they desire, frankly poor or inappropriate. In such cases legal action may be taken and the medical records are always used to judge what actually happened. Also, for patients involved in road traffic accidents, industrial injury or exposed to hazards at work, legal action may ensue and medical information is required. Past medical records are an extremely important source of this information.

For these reasons a medical record must comply with the requirements of a legal document:

Requirements of a Legal Document

- It must be clear to whom the records refer – all documents must display the patient's name, date of birth and hospital number.
- Every entry in the records must be dated and signed. The author of the record must be identifiable. Therefore, you should always use the format: PRINT NAME and designation e.g. 'Senior House Officer' 'Medical Student' etc.
- Any changes in records should be signed and dated.
- No record should be falsified.
- No records should be deleted or removed unless a proper explanation is recorded, signed and dated by the individual responsible for the alteration.
- Medical records must be kept securely and available for inspection by the patient and their legal representatives if required.

WRITING A MEDICAL CASE

As your clinical contact begins, you will no doubt be asked to write and present cases. This chapter details the basic components of a medical case, and describes the rationale behind this approach. There may be variation between the expectation of different clinicians, but in general, all cases have a standard layout. You may choose to document some aspects of the case in greater detail with certain patients. For instance, if a patient presents with knee pain, detailed documentation of the examination of the knee and hip may be included. In other cases, documentation of a GALS screen may be deemed more appropriate.

Basic Patient Details

You should start with the basic details: name, age, sex, date of birth, occupation, marital status, location, admission date, consultant and date of examination. These details are necessary, and asking for them allows you to gently ease the patient into questioning.

E.g.,	Name:	Mr C Clarke (often omitted for confidentiality purposes)
	Age:	58-years-old
	Sex:	Male
	Date of birth:	1/1/1943
	Occupation:	Farmer
	Marital status:	Married
	Location:	Ward 9, St. Elsewhere Hospital
	Hospital Number:	339078
	Date of admission:	10/4/2000
	Consultant:	Dr. X
	Examined on:	12/4/2000

Presenting Complaint

This should be in **the patient's words**, e.g. "I vomited up lots of blood after eating tea". Not: 'post-prandial haematemesis'! It should simply **list each symptom in chronological order** that the patient complains of on admission, along with the **duration of the symptom**.

Presenting complaint

1. Chest pain 2 days (2/7)
2. Shortness of breath 2 weeks (2/52)
3. Ankle swelling 2 months (2/12)
4. Lack of energy 2 years

Initially ask, 'what are you complaining of?' After each symptom is told, ask again, 'any more symptoms' as the patient will often not volunteer all important information. One reason for this is that they may not realise the importance. For example, an elderly lady with profuse diarrhoea may be so preoccupied with the diarrhoea that she fails to tell you that she has lost 2 stones in weight in the last month, has been off her food and noticed blood in her stools. These symptoms would point the diagnosis towards bowel cancer.

History of Presenting Complaint

The history of presenting complaint should be written in a flowing commentary style (prose) in concise paragraphs – using one paragraph for each symptom. It should **start with when the patient was last well**. It should cover all the symptoms in a **chronological fashion** and include any **relevant negative findings** from questions relevant to the presenting complaint. This usually entails questions about the system in which the main complaint is located. For example, if the complaint is of chest pain, negative findings for palpitations, cough, ankle swelling, wheeze etc. should be noted. Again, where possible record the actual words of the patient. Systematic questions mentioned here should not be repeated in the systems review section. It may also be appropriate to document any relevant risk factors in this section.

For example on the week before admission to hospital, the patient noticed increasing dyspnoea, and described 'fighting for a breath.' On some occasions, washing and shaving would leave the patient breathless, and on other days he could walk a small distance before becoming dyspnoeic. The patient also suffers from orthopnoea, requiring three pillows to sleep, but had not experienced paroxysmal nocturnal dyspnoea. He had not noticed a wheeze or cough, and had not produced sputum or had any episodes of haemoptysis. He occasionally experienced central chest tightness if he was walking quickly. This sensation did not radiate anywhere else, and was relieved by rest.

The patient had also noticed that his ankles and legs had been very swollen bilaterally, especially towards the end of the day, in the two weeks before admission to hospital. The patient also noticed they were pale looking before admission. The patient had never experienced any dizzy spells or palpitations. The patient had smoked 20 cigarettes per day for 30 years. He had a myocardial infarction in 1982, and was diagnosed as being hypertensive in 1987. He is not diabetic and did not report hypercholesterolaemia.

After a number of paragraphs each symptom will have been fully explored and the examiner should be in a strong position to construct a differential diagnosis or at least determine which of the main body systems are most likely to be involved in the disease process.

Past Medical History

This is vital, as it allows you to narrow down potential reasons for the acute episode and may indicate the severity of illness by the number of previous admissions to hospital. Also, previous medical intervention may be responsible for the current illness.

For example an elderly patient presenting with symptoms of bowel obstruction may have previously undergone bowel surgery for a colonic carcinoma. This history may indicate a recurrence of cancer, or bowel adhesions which have developed as a consequence of surgery.

Often the patient will not be able to remember some or all of their medical history. Don't forget there are plenty of **alternative sources** if need be: family, friends, neighbours, old medical notes, as well as family doctor and institutional sources (e.g. nursing home, school).

Document the medical (including psychiatric) and surgical admissions in chronological order, with the most recent at the top. Significant medical events not requiring admission should also be noted. This should be recorded as a bulleted list:

- 2000: Coronary artery bypass grafting
- 1999: Diagnosed with angina pectoris
- 1994: Admission for treatment of depression
- 1987: Cholecystectomy
- 1960: Nasal septoplasty

Also record whether or not there is any past history of the common medical disorders that are associated with significant morbidity. These include: ischaemic heart disease, myocardial infarction, tuberculosis, cerebro-vascular accidents, rheumatic fever, diabetes, hypertension, asthma/chronic obstructive airways of disease, epilepsy and jaundice.

Drug History

Accuracy and completeness are paramount in recording what medications a patient receives. Many patients taking several medications carry a list on their person. It is often worth asking to see this. This section should include all current medications, including over the counter preparations, and any significant drugs used in the past such as cytotoxics, immunosuppressants and steroids. Record the drug name, dose, frequency of administration, route of administration and indications.

All medications, with the exception of a few, should be written in their **generic form**, in CAPITAL LETTERS. For example, document OMEPRAZOLE not LOSEC®. Those preparations that include more than one drug or that are special formulations (such as slow or modified release) may need the proprietary (manufacturer's) name to be noted. For example, Adalat® SR is acceptable for the slow release preparation of nifedipine. Medications administered in microgram doses, e.g. digoxin, should have the units written in full (see below). Never use the 'trailing zero' as it can easily result in an overdose of x10 (e.g. 2.0 mg can be mistaken for 20 mg). For drugs given by the frequency PRN (as required), a minimal time interval and/or maximum dose over 24 hours should be recorded.

This section is NOT complete without recording if the patient has any **drug allergies** or has had any previous adverse drug reactions. If there are none, it is convention to write NKDA (no known drug allergies). Ask specifically whether or not the patient is allergic to penicillin.

Drug name	Dose	Frequency	Route	Indication
BISOPROLOL	10 mg	BD	PO	Heart failure
ADALAT® LA	20 mg	OD	PO	Hypertension
COMBIVENT®	20/100 micrograms	TID		COAD
PARACETAMOL	500 mg	PRN 4 hourly	PO	Analgesia
DIGOXIN	125 micrograms	OD	PO	Atrial fibrillation
CO-AMOXYCLAV	125/31 mg in 5ml	TID	PO	Pneumonia

NKDA (no known drug allergies)

When recording medications for children, it is essential that the weight of the child (in kilograms) is recorded clearly. Also for liquid preparations (more commonly used in children) more than one strength may be available. Therefore you should record the strength as shown above for co-amoxiclav.

By convention drug prescription has used Latin terms and abbreviations, such as:

o.d	once daily	p.r.n	when needed
b.d	twice daily	stat	immediately
t.i.d	three times per day	mane	in the morning
q.i.d	four times per day	nocte	at night

Details regarding tobacco use, alcohol use and illicit drug use should also be included here (or alternatively with social and personal history).

Alcohol

Alcohol abuse and alcohol related disease is a major cause of acute and chronic medical illness. It is extremely important to document alcohol intake in a standardised format. The number of units of alcohol consumed per day, week or month should be recorded together with the pattern of alcohol intake i.e. daily alcohol drinker, or a 'binge' drinker. 1 unit of alcohol is ½ pint of beer (standard strength), 1 glass of wine or 1 measure of spirits (25 mls, English pub measure). Therefore for someone who drinks 6 pints of beer and 4 vodkas over a weekend on a regular basis the record would read: **Alcohol – 16 units of alcohol at weekends**.

Smoking

Tobacco use is a major health hazard. Tobacco can be chewed, sniffed (snuff) or inhaled. Cigarette smoking is significantly more harmful than either pipe or cigar smoking. The number of cigarettes smoked each day or the amount (in grammes/ounces) of tobacco used should be recorded. You may get a more accurate value by asking the number of packets/pouches purchased each week as patients invariably underestimate if asked directly. Ask how long they have smoked. If they are a non-smoker, ask if they ever did smoke, and if so how much did they smoke and for how long. These values should then be converted into 'pack years', where one pack year is equivalent to 20 cigarettes a day for one year.

Record of type and amount of tobacco consumed

Smokes
Cigarettes   40 per day for 10 years
Pipe   3 oz per week
Cigar   1–2 per year

Other Drugs

If there is any indication or suspicion, patients should be asked about what are called social/recreational drugs e.g. cannabis, narcotics, amphetamines, glue sniffing.

If these drugs are or have been used, it is vital to inquire about intravenous drug use and whether or not hypodermic needles have been shared. This is relevant because of the risk of infections such as HIV.

Family History

This section is to establish if there is any disease that 'runs in the family' and may be pertinent to the patient's admission. Details of the past or present ill health of parents, siblings, children (if any) and partner should be noted. The ages at which relatives developed ill health, as well as how and when relatives died should be recorded. You may find it useful to construct a family tree, especially if there is a strong family history.

Example
Father, died 15 years ago, aged 56 years, myocardial infarct.
Brother, died 2 years ago, aged 49 years, myocardial infarct.
Brother, aged 47, angina pectoris, diagnosed 6 years ago.

Social and Personal History

This is a vital section for the holistic approach to patient care. This aims to ascertain an insight into a patient's home environment and lifestyle. This is especially important for discharge purposes and for enrolling the help of other members of the healthcare team.

The following essential details should be recorded.

- Ability to perform activities of daily living (transfer, dressing, washing, feeding).

- Location of bedroom and bathroom (e.g. downstairs toilet).
- House type (especially the number of flights of stairs) and any modifications (eg. occupational therapy aids).
- Outside help (eg. meals on wheels, district nurse).
- Family dynamics (who lives at home; any dependants).
- Leisure activities and pets.
- Recent foreign travel.
- Level of education.
- Financial status (especially any benefits received).
- Present and previous occupation(s) and description of work involved.
- Exposure to potentially harmful materials (e.g. asbestos).

Review of Systems

In order that you do not miss any symptoms directly related to the presenting complaint, a review of systems using basic systemic questions should be done. There is no need to repeat the questions asked in the history of presenting complaint.

In order to be efficient and effective in screening medical and surgical patients for illness on admission, one must be able to ask a series of essential questions for each system of the body. These allow one to identify any symptoms suggestive of illness and to elicit symptoms that patients may not readily admit to when asked what troubles them.

On the page overleaf are core general questions. **For any specific system or for any specialist area, many more questions may be asked.** Try to develop a system to remember the questions so they rhyme off without effort, one following the other. For example, for the gastrointestinal system it may help you to think of the gut (from mouth to anus) as one long tube. Start with problems about things going in, such as appetite, weight change and mouth ulcers. Make your way down to the other end, and ask about change in bowel habit, blood passed rectally, and so on.

You might want to keep a copy of these questions in your white coat, especially to begin with, in order that you might become proficient in asking them.

Review of systems

General
Recent weight change
Shivering attacks
Night sweats
Energy levels

Locomotor
Problems with walking
  on flat or stairs
Joints: pain, swelling
  stiffness (morning),
  heat instability.
Muscle weakness
Muscle pain

Skin
Rash
Jaundice
Itch

Genitourinary
Obstructive
  Hesitancy
  Dribbling
  Stranguay
  Altered stream
Irritative
  Dysuria
  Frequency
  Nocturia
  Urgency
Haematuria
Discharge
Last menstrual period
Regularity of periods
Length of period/cycle
Clots
Heaviness of period
  (number of pads)
Age at menarche
Age at menopause
Number of pregnancies

Alimentary
Appetite
Nausea and
  vomiting
Thirst
Mouth ulcers
Dysphagia
Haematemesis
Abdominal pain
Heartburn
Indigestion
Flatulence
Bloating
Bowel habit
Tenesmus
Rectal bleeding
Melaena
Colour of stools
Mucus per rectum
Steatorrhoea

Nervous System
Mood
Weakness
Loss of power
Loss of sensation
Memory
Vertigo
Tinnitus
Dizziness
Balance
Blackouts and fits
Incontinence
Speech disturbances
Paraesthesia
Headaches
Vision
Hearing
Sleeping problems

Cardiorespiratory
Ankle swelling
Palpitations
Chest pain
Syncope
Dyspnoea
Orthopnoea
Paroxysmal nocturnal
Wheezing
Cough
Sputum (quantity,
  consistency, colour)
Haemoptysis
Number of pillows
  required for sleeping
Intermittent
  claudication

Physical Examination

This should entail a basic examination of all systems of the body with **the system demonstrating the main presenting complaint coming first.** Thereafter the order does not really matter, although one general convention is: general, cardiovascular, respiratory, alimentary, nervous, and musculo-skeletal.

The fundamentals of each system should be recorded, including the key negative findings. One of the best ways to see how to do this is to look at some well recorded notes on a general medicine/surgery ward to get a feel for how it is done.

Example – **Respiratory system**

Appearance: breathing comfortably
Sputum: green, sticky, 2 teaspoons a day
Chest shape: normal and symmetrical
Respiratory rate: 18 breaths per minute
Trachea: central
Cricosternal distance: normal
No lymphadenopathy or thyroid disease
Expansion good: right = left
Chest resonant to percussion
Vesicular breath sounds of normal intensity; no adventitious sounds.
Tactile fremitus and vocal fremitus: normal.

Summary

Summarise in one short paragraph the main points of note from the history and examination.

Problem list

List, in order of priority, the problems that should be addressed in the management of the patient.

Example – for a patient admitted with anorexia nervosa: weight loss, poor diet, depression, social problems.

Differential diagnosis

A sensible range of possibilities should be considered, perhaps with some comment justifying why a particular disease has been included. The diseases should be arranged with the most likely coming first.

Investigations

Include a description of the investigations which should be performed, along with relevant results.

Definitive diagnosis

A statement of the most likely disease process, based on the history, physical examination, and investigations.

Management

Details of how the patient should be managed, both in the acute setting, and in the long term.

Commentary

This is included for academic purposes only (i.e. not found in 'real' patient's notes). The expectation of content for the commentary varies considerably between clinicians, and it is a good idea to find out what is expected in this section before you write it. Generally, one aspect of the case is chosen and explored in detail, with reference to medical literature.

✓ *Remember to date, sign and print your position/rank with all medical notes.*

Appendix 1: Example of a Case History

Example of a case history taken by a 3rd year student day/month/year

Patients name	Mrs ER
Occupation	Retired housewife
DOB	19/5/1917
Marital status	Widow with two children

C/O
1. Tiredness – 6/12
2. Weight loss – 3/12
3. Indigestion – 2/12
4. Difficulty swallowing – 2/12
5. Increasing pain on swallowing – 2/52

HPC

Mrs ER first noticed increasing tiredness six months ago leading to increasing rest periods, however she still remains active. Although diagnosed with pernicious anaemia in August, regular injections of B_{12} have not relieved the feeling of tiredness.

She has lost 2 st in the past 3 months which she has attributed to eating less.

'Indigestion' started 2 months ago with a feeling of "burning pain in chest behind breast bone". At first it was precipitated solely by swallowing but in the past two weeks has been constant and exacerbated by swallowing. It is an aching pain which doesn't radiate and is made worse by eating spicy foods, it has no known relieving factors. She has noticed the pain is associated with flatulence, which also causes mild abdominal discomfort.

At the same time the indigestion started Mrs ER noticed difficulty in swallowing. She has more difficulty with meat and solid foods and must chew all food well in order to swallow. Making the swallowing movement itself is not difficult. Fluids are swallowed easiest though they must be swallowed slowly. The neck does not bulge or gargle on drinking.

She has not regurgitated any food nor has she vomited. She has no history of stomach infection. She has been suffering from constipation for the past week though her bowel habit hasn't changed.

Both the pain and difficulty swallowing have caused Mrs ER to eat less, though her appetite has not diminished.

P/H

- Recurrent sinusitis treated with antibiotics as required for over 20 years.
- B_{12} deficiency diagnosed 1 year ago.
- There were no complications in pregnancy or on giving birth.
- There is no history of IHD, diabetes, or hypercholesterolaemia or hypertension.

F/H

- Brother has sinusitis
- No history of IHD, diabetes, hypercholesterolaemia or hypertension
- No history of oesophageal problems
- Cause of death of parents is unknown to patient

S/H

Occupation: Retired housewife
Living conditions: Lives alone in sheltered accommodation, she is a widow with one son (48 year old) and one daughter (41 year old); her daughter visits regularly.
Doesn't smoke or drink.
Can carry out all activities of daily living unaided.
Walks moderate distances regularly and does her own gardening.
Not eating well.

Drug History

Drug	Dose	Route	Frequency	Indication
Lorazepam	2 mg	PO	OD nocte	Sleeping pill
Senna	5 ml	PO	OD nocte	Constipation
Lansoprazole	30 mg	PO	OD mane	Indigestion and heartburn

Not allergic to any medication.

O/E

General inspection
Cachectic woman
Temperature 37.2°C
Tongue clean and moist
Teeth and gums healthy
Absent tonsils, throat not injected
Anaemia of skin and mucous membranes
No cyanosis
No jaundice
No lymphadenopathy
Thyroid not enlarged
No oedema
No finger clubbing

Abdomen
Normal in shape
Moves well with respiration
No tenderness, rigidity or guarding
Liver, kidneys and spleen not palpable
No ascites

Cardiovascular system
Pulse: rate 80, regular, normal character and volume, no thickening of arterial wall
JVP: not visible
Apex beat: 5th intercostal space, mid-clavicular line
No evidence of cardiac enlargement
Heart sounds: S1 + S2 heard in all areas, no murmurs
BP: 140/86 mmHg

Respiratory system
Shape: normal and symmetrical
Movement: good and symmetrical
No impairment of percussion note
Breath sounds vesicular: no adventitious sounds
VR and VF normal

Nervous system
Normal mentality and intelligence
Pupils equal; regular, react equally to L&A

Eye movement not impaired: no nystagmus
Other cranial nerves normal; fundi normal
KJ's and AJ's are present and equal on both sides: PR flexor response

Investigations

FBC (particularly to monitor signs of anaemia): normal
U&E (to ensure normal electrolyte balance as could be affected by malnutrition and disease process): mild urea decrease and mild LDH decrease
Oesophago-gastro-duodenoscopy (OGD) and biopsy (to confirm or exclude – peptic ulcers, or upper GI carcinoma): 4 cm growth at 35 cm. Either anaplastic small cell carcinoma secondary from lung or atypical primary oesophageal carcinoma.
CXR (to view a possible site for primary lung tumour): no chest lesion
CT brain, thorax, abdomen (for volume of tumour and to find evidence of metastases): not done yet
Barium swallow (to assess degree of stricture and size of tumour, also any dilatation or disorders of peristalsis can be seen): not done yet

Diagnosis and Management

Differential diagnoses
These include any cause of dysphagia

- **Malignant**: oesophageal cancer, gastric cancer, pharyngeal cancer, extrinsic pressure from lung cancer
- **Neurological causes**: bulbar palsy, lateral medullary syndrome, myasthenia gravis, syringomyelia
- **Others**: benign strictures, pharyngeal pouch, achalasia, systemic sclerosis, oesophagitis, iron deficiency anaemia

From the history, Mrs ER cannot drink fluids as fast as usual which actually suggests a motility problem such as the neurological causes or achalasia. The lack of difficulty making the swallowing movement rules out bulbar palsy. Since the neck doesn't bulge or gargle on drinking, a pharyngeal pouch is unlikely. The OGD confirms oesophageal tumour. Benign tumours are rare and often symptomless however, while malignant oesophageal cancer is the eighth most common cancer in the world. The biopsy is inconclusive but since the lungs are clear from the CXR the most likely diagnosis is primary oesophageal cancer. The most common types are squamous, which is more common in men, smokers and alcohol drinkers, and adenocarcinoma. It has been noted that the carcinoma of the patient is 'atypical'. The CT scans will be very important in, hopefully, confirming that this is the only site of tumour, and will strongly influence the management of this patient.

Carcinoma of oesophagus occurs mainly in the age range 60–70 years, though the age of onset is dropping. As in this dysphagia is present and progressively gets worse with first difficulty swallowing solids then liquids as well. The lesion often forms a stricture and often invades surrounding structures rather than metastasising widely. Weight loss, as in this patient, is common secondary to dysphagia as well as anorexia. As the tumour progresses and obstruction becomes greater there will be difficulty swallowing saliva, and coughing with aspiration into the lungs is common. Weight loss, anorexia and lymphadenopathy are the three most frequently found signs (Kumar and Clark, 1998), along with retrosternal chest pain and hoarseness.

Management

This depends on age and fitness of the patient and the stage of the disease. There is only a 5% survival rate for this cancer.

Surgery is the best chance for cure. However, it can only be done if the tumour has not infiltrated beyond the oesophageal wall. There is an 80% survival rate for this treatment. Radiotherapy is associated with worse outcomes than surgery but is cheaper and safer. Chemotherapy treatment used is 5FU, cisplatinum and combined chemoradiation. Wobst et al. (1999) believes that chemoradiation followed by surgery is the best method of treatment.

The main treatment, however, is palliative therapy; repeated dilatation or stenting keeps the lumen open to allow liquids and soft foods to be eaten, fizzy drinks can keep the tubes from blocking. Photocoagulation with a laser beam or necrosis using alcohol injections can relieve dysphasia temporarily. One of the more commonly used endoscopic procedures is laser therapy, which provides symptomatic relief with low complication rates. Recurrent dysphagia is a problem necessitating repeated treatment sessions. Self-expanding metal stents offer a high degree of palliation and are associated with fewer complications compared with prosthetic tubes (Siersema et al, 1999).

Nutritional support is also important as well as emotional support. This involves liaison with the dietician to ensure adequate food intake and relatives should be counselled with regards to the patient's condition.

Patient education

At this stage the patient should be advised that a growth has been found in her gullet which has been causing her recent problems with swallowing. It should be made clear that the extent of the problem won't be known until further tests are done, and that this will affect how she is treated. The patient's expectations should be realistic and it is important to explain that the prognosis will probably be poor. Details about possible surgery, radiotherapy etc are not necessary at this stage, since their treatment is still unknown, unless requested by the patient.

Due to the sensitive and distressing nature of the news it may be better to have a close relative along when breaking the news, privacy should be ensured and extra time must be spent to allow the patient to digest the information and have questions answered. It may be necessary to repeat this information at a later date as emotions may cause some details to be forgotten.

References

Clinical Medicine 4th ed. Kumar P and Clark M (1998) WB Saunders.

Oxford Handbook of Clinical Medicine 3rd ed Hope RA, Longmore JM, Hodgetts TJ and Ramrakha PS. Oxford University Press.

Palliation of Malignant Dysphagia from Oesophageal Cancer Siersema PD, Dees J van Blankenstein M. Rotterdam Oesophageal Tumor Study Group. *Scandinavian Journal of Gastroenterology* – Supplement 225:75-84, 1998.

Oesophageal Cancer Treatment Studies, Strategies and Facts Wobst A, Audision RA, Colleoni M, Geraghty JG.: Ann Oncol 1999 Mar; 10(3):359-60.

Index

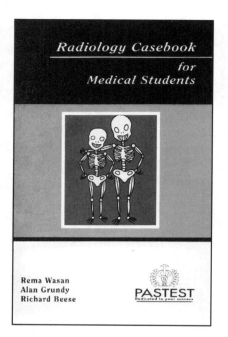